Ormsby M. Mitchel

The Astronomy of the Bible

Ormsby M. Mitchel

The Astronomy of the Bible

ISBN/EAN: 9783337097189

Printed in Europe, USA, Canada, Australia, Japan

Cover: Foto ©Lupo / pixelio.de

More available books at **www.hansebooks.com**

THE

ASTRONOMY OF THE BIBLE.

BY

O. M. MITCHEL, LL.D.,

FORMERLY DIRECTOR OF THE CINCINNATI AND DUDLEY OBSERVATORIES;
AUTHOR OF "PLANETARY AND STELLAR WORLDS," AND "POPULAR
ASTRONOMY;" LATE MAJOR-GENERAL OF U. S. VOLS.

WITH A BIOGRAPHICAL SKETCH.

NEW YORK:
BLAKEMAN & MASON,
No. 21 MURRAY STREET

1863.

PROF. MITCHEL'S BOOKS.

PLANETARY AND STELLAR WORLDS.
1 vol. 12mo. Price, $1 50. Illustrated.

POPULAR ASTRONOMY.
1 vol. 12mo. Price, $1 50. Illustrated.

ASTRONOMY OF THE BIBLE.
1 vol. 12mo. Price, $1 25. With steel portrait.

Entered, according to Act of Congress, in the year 1863, by
E. W. MITCHEL,
In the Clerk's Office of the District Court of the United States for the Southern District of New York.

SMITH & McDOUGAL, Electrotypers.

C. S. WESTCOTT & Co., Printers.

CONTENTS.

LECTURE I.

ASTRONOMICAL EVIDENCES OF THE BEING OF A GOD.

                                                                                            PAGE

The Distinct Character of this Investigation: the Grandeur of the Theme.—Does the Physical Universe proclaim the Being of a God?—Is the God thus revealed the same august and eternal Being portrayed in our Sacred Books?—The Three Hypotheses concerning the Existence of the Universe: first, the Eternity of the Structure; second, the Eternity of Matter, but its Forms and Perpetuity dependent upon Chance; third, a Creative God.—The first untenable; all Nature gives token of Origin and Growth. There is no Eternity in Man, Animal, or Vegetable; nor can there be in the existent Structure of the Universe.—The second proved impossible, by the very act of Reasoning which is necessary to analyze Nature's Laws.—The third Hypothesis clearly stated, and the Discussion begun.—The Argument from Analogy teaches us that a Supreme Intelligence must have made and must now control this Universe.—The Sun, the System, the Mighty Complication, the delicate and complete Adjustment of Parts, the Earth, all indicate this.—Still more striking is the Proof when we pass to the Consideration of the Stars and the other great Systems.................... 47

LECTURE II.

THE GOD OF THE UNIVERSE IS JEHOVAH.

The God of the Bible: His Power and Majesty as He declares them.—Science must accord with Scripture in manifesting Him.—Does the Universe declare the *Unity* of God?—Every Day's Development of Astronomy gives new Proofs of it, in the perfect Harmony which pervades this complex System.—The *Omnipotence* of God likewise taught by this Investigation, in the Creation of these Worlds, in their systematic Arrangement, in now holding them in their Orbits, and compelling them to execute His Will. —His Supreme *Wisdom* likewise displayed in all His Plans, and in the perfect Adjustment of all the Parts of the Great System.—His *Unchangeableness* deduced from this Examination.—His *Omnipresence* established. —His Glory manifested at every step.—Summary.—Whence did the Scripture Writers derive their Knowledge of God ?—The Voice of Nature proclaims God.. 85

LECTURE III.

THE COSMOGONY AS REVEALED BY THE PRESENT STATE OF ASTRONOMY.

The wonderful Character of the Bible: its fearless Self-exposure to Attack; —its "Ethereal Mold, incapable of Stain."—Compared with Classic Writings on Philosophy and Ethics.—Their decay; its perennial Freshness.— The Nebular Hypothesis of Herschel.—La Place's Theory.—The supposed atheistical Tendencies.—Truth never shrinks from the Light.—Herschel's Experiments. The Nebulæ separated; others discerned. The Zodiacal Light.—La Place's Application of the Nebular Hypothesis.—Motion of Rotation.—Great Rings condensing into Orbs.—Difficult Questions: Forces: Principles of their Action.—Will this Theory coincide with the Mosaic Account of the Creation.. 128

LECTURE IV.

THE MOSAIC ACCOUNT OF CREATION, COMPARED WITH THE COSMOGONY OF THE UNIVERSE AS REVEALED IN THE ACTUAL CONDITION OF ASTRONOMY.

Analysis of the Words of Moses which explain the Creation, "In the Beginning;" "The Heavens and the Earth," etc.: the Language scanned.—Milton's Fiction concerning Light.—What was this Light which God thus called into Being ?—The *Days* of Creation.—The *Firmament*.—The Second great Epoch finished —The Third Epoch: the Gathering of the Waters and the Appearance of the Land.—The Existence of Vegetable Life without a Sun. The Fourth Epoch: the *Great Lights*, "for Signs and for Seasons, for Days and for Years."—The simple Record not intended as distinct Astronomical Revelation.—The Creation of Man.—No complete Demonstration intended, only an approximate one............. 173

LECTURE V.

AN EXAMINATION OF THE ASTRONOMICAL ALLUSIONS IN THE BOOK OF JOB.

The Authorship of the Book: its Antiquity; its wonderful Statements.— God's Answers to Job considered.—Nicer Shades of Meaning in Translation.—The Bounds of the Ocean.—The Dayspring from on High.—Tides.— The Ocean's Limits fixed while Day and Night endure.—Hesiod's Fancy.— Other striking Queries.—Further Consideration of Light.—The Littleness of Human Science.. 213

LECTURE VI.

THE ASTRONOMICAL MIRACLES OF THE BIBLE MIRACLES OF POWER.

Such an Inquiry not within our Scope—Astronomy deals with the Phenomena of Nature, not the Miracles of God.—The Subject, however, may be in some degree illustrated.—The Universe governed by invariable Laws.—These Miracles seem to suspend them.—The Stopping of the Sun and Moon at Joshua's Command, and the Going backward of the Shadow on the Sundial of Ahaz.—Difficulties of the Subject.—Can God work Miracles?—What is a Miracle?—The new Elijah.—The Case of Joshua considered.—How can that Miracle be accounted for?—By stopping the Rotation of the Earth on its Axis.—Can this be done without universal Derangement?—Are we to suppose that God would do it?—If asserted as done, can we credit it?— Yes.—Refraction miraculously applied.—The Miracle of the Sun-dial of Ahaz may thus be accounted for.—Further Details of Joshua's Success.—A probable Interpolation.—What astronomic Research can discover.—Suppose the Investigation made, it could only concern the Rotation of the Earth.—The Effect of stopping the Rotation.—The New Testament Prophecies as to the End of the Earth.—Man's Ignorance a Reason for Reverence and Faith.—We know that God lives and speaks, and this is all we need to know.—The Superiority of the Moral to the Material.................. 249

LECTURE VII.

THE LANGUAGE OF THE BIBLE.

The Language of the Bible a Proof of its Inspiration.—It differs from that of other Oriental Nations, who saw the same Splendors of the Heavens.—The first Sentence in the Bible.—"In the Beginning God created the Heavens and the Earth."—A grand Assertion.—No Argument.—The Egyptian Fancy of the Origin of the Creation.—The Persian.—The Views of Thales; of Plato; of Aristotle; of Zeno; of Epicurus.—A further Consideration of the Mosaic Account.—God's Providence displayed.—Modern Science can only begin where Moses left off.—The Lawgiver and the Laws.—Undevout Astronomers few in comparison to the Devout;—Copernicus, Kepler, Tycho, Galileo, Newton.— Quotations from the Old Testament Writers.—Their Language the only fitting Vehicle for the overwhelming Thoughts.—Their Declarations examined.—The Orbit of Neptune.—The Milky Way.—The Habit of using the Language of the Bible causes us to forget its Grandeur and Appositeness.—Specific Declarations examined; Day and Night; the Ocean's Bounds.—Beyond our System.—Bessel's Observations.—The Foundations of the Earth "Upon Nothing;" Hung in empty Space; Established forever.—St. Paul on Mars' Hill.—Points in his Discourse unanswerable.—Striking Illustration of a rebellious Planet.—God's Goodness... 283

PREFACE.

THE volume here offered to the public contains the last finished astronomical work of Professor Mitchel; and, with those that he published before his death, constitutes a series which, if not exhaustive of the accepted divisions of the science, presents, in outline, its great physical features and its ethical relations. "The Planetary and Stellar Worlds," published in 1848, contained a popular exposition of the important discoveries and splendid theories of modern astronomy. It traced the progress of the great science from the primitive ages, showing how, little by little, the true theory dawned upon the feeble mind of man, fearful and long unwilling to receive it; it presented the great laws, with copious and eloquent illustration; it offered clear solutions of the wondrous problems; discussed the discovery of new planets and the characteristics of the cometary world; displayed the grandeur of the scale upon which the universe is built, and showed the benevolent provisions for its permanent stability.

The "Popular Astronomy," published in 1860, is a concise elementary treatise on our sun, planets, satellites, and comets; bringing the lofty truths and mighty laws within the scope of popular and youthful comprehension. It is at once lucid and eloquent, and serves admirably as a manual of instruction.

The present work is of an entirely different nature from both these, but in some sort complementary to them. As a devout Christian man, Professor Mitchel was aware of the difficulties which beset the honest seeker for truth, by reason of the neological arguments of the free-thinker, based upon an apparent want of harmony between modern astronomy and the Bible; and he determined to apply his great practical knowledge to a popular exposition of this subject. The day seemed to have passed when the careless crowd would allow the truth of the assertion, "The undevout astronomer is mad;" and he bent his energies to such a work as should extort the confession once more from all who heard, or should read him. He always intended doubtless, to put these lectures in a book form, but they were originally delivered before large audiences in many of our principal cities, with the happiest effect; confirming the faith of many, and arousing the devotion of all.

But they were never more timely than now. The exploded gnosticism of Germany has made its way into England; has invaded the English Church and assumed our English speech. Essayists and reviewers first strike the secret blow; and then an English bishop attacks the faith once delivered to the saints, with weapons forged in her own armories, and turned against her by her traitors and deserters. Professor Mitchel's work is no designed answer to Bishop Colenso's cavils and sophistries—for it was prepared before the bishop had started upon his meteoric course; but it certainly is strangely providential that, while an English prelate, whose sworn duty it is to defend the Church, smites it with parricidal hand, an American astronomer, who, in the following of many of his scientific co-workers, might have been expected to doubt, or, at the least, to be supremely indifferent, rises from his grave, as it were, to confront him with a chastened, instructed, and devout belief, and to answer his shallow learning with words of "truth and soberness."

Those who look in this volume, however, for an arrogant demonstration of positive harmony between astronomy and the Bible, will be disappointed: its author does not pretend to make out a case. The proof of perfect harmony can only be found in the full development of science; it can only be stated now as an increasing probability. The earlier stages of science presented singular apparent errors in the Scripture accounts: as science has progressed, many of the discrepancies have disappeared; every day throws new light into dark places; and, as difficulty after difficulty is cleared away, we reason, not illogically, to a time when this perfect harmony shall be morally demonstrated. When the nebular hypothesis of Herschel, and the consequent investigations of Laplace, were first brought to light, they were regarded as an impious attempt upon the Mosaic account of the creation: it was a prejudged case; no orthodox Christian, not an educated astronomer, dared to examine them, hardly, indeed, to glance at them; and yet, Professor Mitchel, boldly accepting the scientific investigations and deductions of these astronomers as worthy of careful examination, has given a brilliant elucidation of the Bible narrative by their means;

and in the light thus thrown upon the subject, we see new elements of a harmony which time alone can perfect.

By means of a few pages he has left, in fragmentary form, we know that it was his purpose to continue this subject by considering the relations of astronomy to Christianity, or the harmony of the science with the record of the New Testament. From this fragment a few lines may be quoted. After giving, in rapid summary, the points discussed in these lectures, he says:

"Admitting that we have been successful in exhibiting the above facts under a light satisfactory to the thoughtful and candid, there still remains the grand question, that that Almighty Being who created all things by the word of His power, who hath built the universe in wisdom, who inhabiteth eternity, who filleth immensity by His presence, who is the same yesterday, to-day, and forever,—could have condescended to clothe Himself with the garments of humanity, to suffer indignity and insult, and injury and death, at the hands of His own creatures, upon this globe that we inhabit, which itself is but an atom in the infinite empire of the ever-living God.

" To the candid searcher after truth, who is willing to be convinced; who is anxious to believe the great mystery of God manifest in the flesh; who would gladly accept the doctrine of an infinite Saviour dying upon the cross to atone for the sins of mortals, here, undoubtedly, will be found a difficulty far greater than all others hitherto considered, and rising far above them all in power and resistance.

" It would not be fair, therefore, to close our investigation and end the discussion without an attempt, feeble as it may be, to elucidate this last great subject. I know the theme is difficult; I comprehend fully the nature of the task I am about to undertake; and while I can not hope to remove doubt from the mind of any one, I may yet venture to suggest a train of thought which, if carried to its legitimate results, may lead the struggling mind out of the dim regions of doubt into the clear atmosphere of faith and hope."

We may regret that he was unable to complete this grand investigation; for as Christianity is the prophetic purpose and end of the Old Testament scriptures, so all science must be made to harmonize not simply with the older record, but with the perfected plan of man's redemption.

Deploring, as we do, the country's loss in the death of so energetic and skillful a general, it is to be observed that, as a man of science, his death was especially premature. As he entered the army purely and solely from patriotic motives, he would doubtless have left it immediately upon the announcement of an honorable peace, and gone back with an ardor sharpened by his forced relinquishment of science, to his astronomical studies. He had, to all human appearance, a brilliant future still before him. He was still, at the time of his death, director of both the observatories, at Cincinnati and Albany, and found time, amid his military duties, to send instructions to the assistants in charge, and to keep himself acquainted with the condition of the institutions.

BIOGRAPHICAL NOTICE.

THE subject of this sketch, and the distinguished author of the following pages, had achieved such brilliant success in science and in arms, that the detailed story of his life would be read with eager interest by his admiring countrymen. It is to be hoped that such a biography will not be withheld; not alone in eulogy of his virtues and his achievements, but as a bright example to ourselves and to our children. It is not, however, the purpose of the writer, here and now, to present these details. In offering to the world his lectures on the Astronomy of the Bible, as a posthumous publication, it is only intended to glance, in this preliminary sketch, at the principal objective points in that eager, ardent, devout, and energetic life, as a fitting exordium to those last and fervently pious words which, he being "dead, yet speaketh": thus to present to the reader the lecturer with his lectures; to show what manner of man he was who thus rushes ardently, armed with scientific research, to the support of the faith so variously attacked, and apparently imperiled, in this day of more than Athenian novelties and curiosity.

ORMSBY MCKNIGHT MITCHEL was born in Union County, Kentucky, on the 28th of August, 1810. He had the misfortune to lose his father when he was three years old, and thus from his early infancy he was left to battle with the world, and win such a place in its esteem as the God-given genius and indomitable energy he possessed might secure for him. Immediately after his father's death his family removed to Ohio; and at twelve years of age he became a clerk in a store in the town of Miami, from whence, however, not long after, he moved with his family to Lebanon. A bright and inquiring boy, he soon found the plodding and menial duties of a country store tame, painful, and unsatisfactory.

Always eager in the pursuit of learning, and especially of that practical knowledge which could clear the wilderness and build towns like magic in our then wild as well as far West, he bent his energies toward procuring an appointment to the Military Academy at West Point, where, he had been told, such instruction was given at the expense of the government, and an assured future lay beyond to the honorable graduate. He was successful; he entered the Military Academy on the 23d of June, 1825, when not yet fifteen years old—being admitted, by special favor, a year earlier than the law allowed. His standing while a cadet was always high; and his pursuit of knowledge, in all its forms, eager and persevering. Among his classmates were the most distinguished generals at present in our own or the rebel service; among the latter were Lee and Joseph Johnston. His letters to his mother and brother during this period all represent him as an eager student and ambitious in his aims.

In 1829 he graduated with honor, and was appointed a second lieutenant in the second artillery. So favorable was the impression produced by his novitiate, that he was very soon detailed for duty at the academy, as Assistant Professor of Mathematics. He was afterward, for a short time, stationed at St. Augustine, in Florida. But the prospects of the army at that period could not satisfy the energy and honorable ambition of such a man as Mitchel. He resigned on the 30th of September, 1832, with no fortune, and no prospect but in persevering labor to achieve fame, usefulness, and honor.

It is worthy of record, as illustrative of his character, that just after his graduation the French Revolution broke out;—those "three days of July" which drove the "legitimate" Bourbons once more from the throne they were unworthy to occupy, and elevated the citizen-king, Louis Philippe, to the seat of power. Many remember the effect produced by this volcanic eruption all over the civilized world. Our young soldier was not exempt from the pervading influence. His letters to his brother express an unsettled condition of mind, and a growing desire to go to Europe and plunge, sword in hand, into the great wars which he believed would grow out of this change of dynasty. This is mentioned as betokening his quickly-kindled enthusiasm, his desire to exercise his newly-acquired powers, and his ardent but honorable ambition for distinction. The spirit of revolution which France evoked, and which stalked for a brief space through Europe, was soon laid, and Mitchel settled, as has been told, into the quiet but hard-working life of a citizen.

While in the army he had married Mrs. Trask, the widow of Lieutenant Trask, and formerly Miss Louisa Clark, of Cornwall, on the Hudson. In his growing family he found new incentives to labor; and so we see him, in 1832, opening an office as counsellor-at-law in Cincinnati. In this position he remained until the establishment of the Cincinnati College in 1834, when he was elected Professor of Mathematics, Philosophy, and Astronomy. This post he held until the sad and untimely destruction of the college buildings by fire, and the consequent dissolution of the college. But what seemed his misfortune was in reality a great blessing. In the routine of academic duties he might have remained satisfied; but when once more thrown upon his own remarkable energies, his "sleepless soul" undertook grand and original adventures.

During the period of his professorship he could still

find time to devote to other public duties. From 1836 to 1837 he was chief engineer of the Little Miami Railroad. He had, while in the army, acquired some experience in railway engineering, which was to prove of value on many occasions during his life of peace, and to find brilliant illustrations during his brief but splendid military career. But his principal study was astronomy, the objective science which kindled his ardor and claimed all his devotion. Amid the drudgery of the lawyer's office; while teaching the elements of mathematics and mechanics; in the practical, busy life of a railway engineer, the stars shone upon him with that potent *influence* with which in earlier days they had been supposed to shine upon every man. For him, we may almost believe, there was a horoscope, and that all the planets were conjoined in its composition.

In 1842 he undertook to establish the Cincinnati Observatory—now The Mitchel Observatory—a gigantic labor, which would have been too much for talent, energy, and industry less than his own. Of the difficulties which he encountered we may best judge by his own narrative. Writing, in 1848, he says: "My attention had been for many years directed to this subject (the erection of a great astronomical observatory in the city of Cincinnati), by the duties of the professorship, which I then held in the college. In attempting to communicate the great truths of astronomy, there were no instruments at hand to confirm and fix the wonderful facts recorded in the books. Up to that period our country, and the West particularly, had given but little attention to practical astronomy. A few individuals, with a zeal and ardor deserving of all praise, had struggled on to eminence almost without means or instruments. An isolated telescope was found here and there scattered through the country; but no regularly organized observatory, with powerful instruments, existed within the limits of the United States, so far as I know. * * *

"To ascertain whether any interest could be excited in the public mind in favor of astronomy, in the spring of 1842 a series of lectures was delivered in the hall of the Cincinnati College. To give an increased effect to these discourses (which were unwritten, and in a style of great simplicity), a mechanical contrivance was prepared, by the aid of which the beautiful telescopic views in the heavens were presented to the audience, with a brilliancy and power scarcely inferior to that displayed by the most powerful telescopes. To this fortunate invention were these lectures ('The Planetary and Stellar Worlds'), no doubt, principally indebted for the interest which they produced, and which occasioned them to be attended by a very large number of the intelligent persons in the city. Encouraged by the large audiences, which continued through two months to fill the lecture-room, and still more by the request to repeat the last lecture of the course in one of the great churches of the city, I matured a plan for the building of an observatory, which it was resolved should be presented to the audience at the close of the lecture, in case circumstances should favor. * * *

"In Europe, imperial treasure and princely munificence could build the temples of science; under a free government no such means existed, and to accomplish the erection of these great scientific institutions, the intelligent liberality of the whole community was the only resource. But it had been denied that this resource could be relied on; and it had been roundly asserted that, in the nature of things, the United States must ever remain grossly defective in all the appliances for scientific research. To test the truth or falsehood of these statements was not a difficult matter; and thus encouraged by the interest already manifested in behalf of astronomy, I had already resolved to devote *five* years of faithful effort to accomplish the erection of a great astronomical observatory in the city of Cincinnati.

"This announcement was received with every mark of favor, and the following simple plan was at once presented. The entire amount required to erect the buildings and purchase the instruments, should be divided into shares of twenty-five dollars; every shareholder to be entitled to the privileges of the observatory, under the management of a board of control, to be elected by the shareholders. Before any subscription should become binding, the names of three hundred subscribers should be first obtained. This accomplished, these three hundred should meet, organize, and elect a board, who should thenceforward manage the affairs of the association.

"Such is the history of the origin of the Cincinnati Astronomical Society. * * *

"On the second day I started for New York, and on the 16th of June, 1842, sailed for Liverpool. Having visited many of the best appointed observatories both in England and on the continent (in each and every one of which I was received with a degree of kindness and attention for which I acknowledge the deepest obligations), and having been unsuccessful in finding, either in London or Paris, an object-glass of the size required, I finally determined to visit the city of Munich. The fame of the optical institute of the celebrated Frauenhofer had even reached the banks of the Ohio; and it was hoped that, in that great manufactory, an instrument such as the society desired might be obtained, if not completed, at least in such a state of forwardness as to permit it to be furnished at an early day. In this I was not disappointed. An object-glass of nearly twelve inches diameter, and of superior finish, was found in the cabinet of M. Mertz, the successor of Frauenhofer. This glass had been subjected to a severe trial in the tube of the great refractor of the Munich observatory, by

Dr. Lamont, and had been pronounced of the highest quality.

"To mount this glass would require about two years, at a cost of nearly ten thousand dollars; a sum considerably greater than that appropriated at the time for an equatorial telescope. Having made a conditional arrangement for this and other instruments, I returned to Greenwich, England, where, at the invitation of Professor Airy, the Astronomer Royal, I remained for some time to study. Having accomplished the objects of my journey, I returned home, and rendered a report to a very large meeting of the members of the association and other citizens of Cincinnati. * * *

"The principal instrument having been ordered, and the first payment on its cost made, attention was now given to the procuring of a suitable site for the building. Fortunately for the society, the place of all others most perfectly adapted to their wants, was then the property of Nicholas Longworth, Esq. It is a lofty hill-top, rising some four hundred feet above the level of the city, and commanding a perfect horizon in all directions. On making known to Mr. Longworth the prospects and wants of the Astronomical Society, the writer was directed by him to select *four acres* on the hill-top, out of a tract of some twenty-five acres, and to proceed at once to enclose it, as it would give him great pleasure to present it to the association. On compliance with the conditions of the title-bond, a deed has since been received, placing the society in full possession of this elegant position.

"Preparations were now made to commence the erection of the building for the observatory. The grounds were enclosed, a road built, rendering access to the hill-top comparatively easy, the excavations for the foundations were made, and, on the 9th day of November, 1843, the corner-stone of the pier which was to sustain the great Refracting Telescope was laid by *John Quincy Adams*, with appropriate ceremonies. On this occasion Mr. Adams made his last great oration. The deep interest which he had taken in astronomical science warranted the hope that he might be induced to visit the West on the occasion of laying the foundation-stone of the first great popular observatory ever erected in the United States. This hope was not disappointed. The unaffected devotion of this truly great man to the interests of his country, were, perhaps, never more perfectly exhibited than in his ready acquiescence to comply with the wishes of the Astronomical Society, that he should perform for them the important services on which the future success of this new enterprise in no small degree depended. His high character, his advanced age, the length of the journey, the inclemency of the season, all combined to exhibit to his countrymen the depth of his interest in a cause which could induce such sacrifices.

"After the laying of the corner-stone, the lateness of

the season, and other causes, induced a suspension of the work on the building for the winter; and it was not resumed until May, 1844. In the mean time, after incredible difficulty, the entire amount called for in the payment for the great telescope, was collected and remitted; and the society was left with scarcely a dollar of available means, to commence the erection of a building which, according to the plan, would cost some seven or eight thousand dollars."

* * * * * * * *

"At length, however, the building was reared, and finally covered in, without incurring any debt. But the conditions of the bond, by which the lot of ground was held, required the completion of the observatory in two years from its date; and these two years would expire in June, 1845. It was seen to be impossible to carry forward the building fast enough to secure its completion by the required time, without incurring some debt. My own private resources were used, in the hope that a short time after the finishing of the observatory would be sufficient to furnish the funds to meet all engagements. The work was pushed rapidly forward. In February, 1845, the great telescope safely reached the city of Cincinnati; and in March the building was ready for its reception. I had now exhausted all my private means, and, to increase the difficulty of the position in which I was placed, the College edifice took fire and burned to the ground. My ordinary means of support were thus destroyed at a single blow. I had engaged to conduct the observatory, without compensation from the society, for ten years, in the hope that my college salary would be sufficient for my wants. It was impossible to abandon the observatory. The college could not be rebuilt, at least for several years, and in this emergency I found it necessary to seek some means of support, least inconsistent with my duties in the observatory. My public lectures at home had been comparatively well received, and after much hesitation it was resolved to make an experiment elsewhere. For five years I had been pleading the cause of science among those little acquainted with its technical language. I had become habituated to the use of such terms as were easily understood; and probably to this circumstance, more than to any other one thing, am I indebted for any success which may have attended my public lectures. To the citizens of Boston, Brooklyn, New York, and New Orleans, for the kindness with which they were pleased to receive my imperfect efforts, I am deeply indebted. My lectures were never written, and no idea was entertained of publishing a course, until the partiality of my friends induced me to attempt this experiment."

Thus it was that in 1842 he began his remarkable career as a lecturer on astronomy. More than any other man in America has he thus accomplished for his favor-its science: besides the observatory he founded, and the instruments he imported—and to which he has greatly added by his improvements and inventions—he awakened in thousands of minds an interest in the subject, instructed popular assemblies, not only by his clear outlines of the gigantic science, but by his masterly handling of its difficult and abstruse theories and problems, and by his fiery words, which, exhibiting his own knowledge and enthusiasm, told of its divine beauties and relations, and kept crowded audiences all over the country in breathless and delighted attention.

He had surveyed the Ohio and Mississippi Railroad in 1844; and when the enterprise was fairly undertaken and the road placed under contract, he was sent to Europe by the Company, as a confidential agent on the business of the road, in 1853; and again, on the same business, in 1854. For some time he was connected with the Eastern division of that road, and was chiefly instrumental in bringing it to a successful completion.

In the summer of 1860 he was appointed Director of the Dudley Observatory; and without a reference to the unhappy difficulties which beset that institution at the beginning, it may be said that his acceptance of the post restored quiet, and produced the greatest usefulness of which the observatory was instrumentally and financially capable. It was still under his direction at the time of his death.

When the war broke out, Professor Mitchel, urged singly and purely by patriotic motives, placed his services at the disposition of the government, and devoted his life and military knowledge to his country. On the 9th of August, 1861, he was appointed a Brigadier-General of Volunteers, and was placed in command of the Department of the Ohio, with his head-quarters at Cincinnati. While there he carefully surveyed the approaches to the town, built redoubts and projected lines at the prominent points, which doubtless served a good purpose when, at a later day, Cincinnati was threatened by an overwhelming rebel force.

When the Departments of the Ohio and the Cumberland were afterward united, General Mitchel was ordered to report to General Buell; and he was then placed in command of a camp of rendezvous, where he was actively receiving, organizing, and forwarding troops for three weeks. At the expiration of this brief period he was appointed to the command of the *third* division of the Army of the Ohio, then stationed at Elizabetown, Kentucky. If we particularize in dates and positions, it is that the reader may trace the rapid and energetic movements of General Mitchel the more intelligibly.

On the 9th of February, 1862, he was at Bacon Creek; on the 13th he started for Bowling Green, until then the strongest point on the strategic line of the rebel army. Forced marches, in themselves a wonderful feat with new troops, brought him to Bowling Green on the 15th. On the 22d he started, with General Buell, for Nashville; and it is worth recording that that city was surrendered to Colonel Kennett, of the Fourth Ohio Cavalry, for General Mitchel, on Sunday evening, February 23. The surrender is publicly believed to have been made to General Nelson. But that officer did not arrive with his division to occupy the place until three days after it had capitulated to General Mitchel. He had now entered upon those brilliant independent movements which had excited the admiration of the whole country, and which, could he have received timely and adequate reënforcements, would have redeemed the entire region in which they were made. Early in March he was at Murfreesboro', where, putting his railroad experience into practice, he improvised twelve hundred feet of bridges. Leaving Murfreesboro' on the 6th of April, he marched to Shelbyville; on the 10th he was at Fayetteville; and on the 11th at Huntsville, in Alabama. Here, again, the railway engineer supplied valuable generalship. Seizing the rolling stock, he immediately sent out two railway expeditions, east and west—the one to Decatur, and the other to Stevenson, on the Memphis and Charleston Railroad. The expedition to Stevenson he conducted in person. Both places were captured, and Northern Alabama was in Federal possession, one hundred and twenty miles of the railroad being in running condition, and guarded by Mitchel's troops.

For this brilliant achievement he was made a Major-General of Volunteers, to date from April 11, the day of the capture of Huntsville.

On the 2d of July, General Mitchel was ordered to report himself at Washington. He was there in person on the 5th. From that time he was waiting for orders until September 12th, when he started for the important command of the Tenth Army Corps, the head-quarters of which were at Hilton Head, South Carolina. He reached there on the 16th. His coming infused new life into the department; and he was maturing his plans for a grand movement when he was called away from earth. He sent an expedition to the St. John's River, which captured the fort, with many heavy guns; and also a force to Pocotaligo, for the purpose of destroying the Charleston and Savannah Railroad and telegraph, in which it was successful. He also drew Beauregard out of Savannah with twenty-five thousand men. What he further intended can not be told; but every day, had he lived, would have disclosed the character of his projects, of which these movements were but the initiation.

While in the midst of his usefulness and rapidly-maturing plans, he was attacked by the yellow fever on Sunday, the 26th of October, and died on October 30, 1862, in Beaufort, S. C.

Such, briefly, is the record of his life: the meagre recital is full of valuable lessons, and leads the scholar, the patriot, the soldier, and the Christian to moralize upon the great loss the country has sustained, while they eulogize his genius, his talents, his virtues, his piety, and his lofty achievements. Few men of our age have exhibited a more extended genius; and we know of no one who has displayed so much energy in every thing he has undertaken. His character will bear minute analysis: in every department of labor he was eminently successful; in many he was truly great.

As a *man of science* Professor Mitchel was an ardent investigator and an eminently practical inventor. Fully imbued with the poetry of science, delighting in the lofty picturesques of astronomic thought, abounding in the rarest imagery in his public teachings, his truest sphere was in the mechanism of the means for scientific observation and labor. To prepare himself as director of the observatory, he had studied and mastered the higher astronomical mathematics, and was thoroughly conversant with the history of the science. To qualify himself as a public teacher, he had resolved the most difficult problems into such simple forms and such lucid language as to make them clear to many who had regarded it impossible to comprehend them. To give himself facility in observing, he had studied under Professor Airey, the Astronomer Royal of England, at

Greenwich; and to understand the scientific relations of astronomy as they appear in the cosmogony of the universe, he had investigated those sister sciences which, while they are distinct elements of the great subject, come forward, in harmonious concourse, to cast their tribute at the feet of Him who dictated the record of Moses.

As a mechanical inventor he may be best presented by placing in this connection some account of the principal instruments which he created, for facilitating observations.

The following description of the Declinometer is furnished through the kindness of Mr. G. W. Hough, the astronomer in charge of the Dudley Observatory:

"*Method invented by Professor Mitchel for determining difference of Declination.*

"The apparatus for observing difference of declination consists of the following:

"To the axis of the transit telescope is attached a metallic arm of sixty inches in length; in the lower end of this arm is screwed a cylindrical pin one eighth of an inch in diameter, at right angles to the arm and parallel to the supporting axis of the telescope. This pin has a notch or groove (of the form which would be generated by placing the vertices of two isosceles triangles together and revolving about the perpendicular) cut in the middle.

"At a distance of twenty-three inches from the pin, and in the same horizontal plane, is mounted in Y's a small telescope of six inches focal length. The supporting axis of this telescope is parallel to that of the transit. Underneath the center of the small telescope, and connected with it, is a short arm two inches in length; and, by means of a joint, a rod is connected with the pin before mentioned.

"Now when the transit telescope is moved in zenith-distance, angular motion is given to the small telescope by means of the long arm and connecting rod.

"The amount of this motion is read from a scale, placed at a distance of fifteen feet, and divided to single seconds of arc. It will, of course, be understood that we must have some object in the focus of the small telescope with which to compare the divisions of the scale. We use either a cross formed by the intersection of two spider's webs, or a single horizontal wire.

"In case we wish to observe a zone of greater width than the extent of the scale (30'), we have a number of pins, at distances of 30' apart, mounted in the arc of a circle whose radius is equal to the length of the long arm. We readily pass from one pin to another, by lifting one end of the connecting rod and attaching it to a different one. The divisions on the scale can easily be read, by estimation, to two tenths of a second of arc.

"The time required to read the scale is much less than that employed in reading *one* microscope, since at the same transit of an equatorial star we can make from ten to fifteen bisections and readings. As I have found one reading of the scale nearly equal to four microscopes, it follows that if we employ the same time in the observation of an object with the Declinometer that we do when we use the Circle, our results in the former case will be superior to the latter in a large ratio.

"The Zone observations with the Declinometer have been made mostly for the investigation of the source and amount of error due to this method. From a comparison of the observations with those made in the ordinary way, I find the probable error, on a single observation, falls within the limits of accuracy usually assigned to observations made with the Meridian Circle. One great advantage lies in the fact that many bisections and readings can be made at the same transit, and in this way eliminating the ordinary errors of observation. You will understand the rapidity with which work can be done by this method, when I state that more than two hundred stars have been accurately observed in one hour; and were they equally distributed, twice that number could easily have been taken.

"This instrument is one of the great inventions of our late and lamented director, Professor Mitchel; and is the only one in the world.

"From observations made during the last two years, and a careful discussion of the results, I have arrived at the conviction *that there is no other known method equal to it, for rapidity and accuracy, in the cataloguing of stars."*

Professor Mitchel's remarkable mechanical skill, his quickness to perceive difficulties, and the readiness with which he devised and applied the remedies, are further admirably illustrated in his apparatus for recording time by means of the electro-magnetic telegraphs. These are now in use in the Cincinnati and Dudley Observatories. His was the first thorough solution of this important problem in instrumental astronomy. The following account of this apparatus is in Professor Mitchel's own words :

"The problem of causing a clock to record its beats telegraphically, was nothing more than to contrive some method whereby the clock might be made (by the use of some portion of its own machinery) to take the place of the finger of the living, intelligent operator, and "make" or "break" the electric circuit. The grand difficulty did not lie in causing the clock to play the part of an automaton in this precise particular, but it did lie in causing the clock to act automatically, and at the same time perform perfectly its great function of a time-keeper. This became a matter of great difficulty and delicacy; for to tax any portion of the clock machinery with a duty beyond the ordinary and contemplated demands of the maker, seemed at once to involve the machine in imperfect and irregular action. After due reflection it was decided to apply to the *pendulum* for a minute amount of power, whereby the making or breaking the electric circuit might be accomplished with the greatest chance of escaping any injurious effect on the going of the clock. The principle which guided in this selection was, that we ought to go to the prime mover (which in this case was the clock weights, and which could not be employed), and, failing to reach the prime mover, we should select the nearest piece of mechanism to it, which in the clock is the pendulum. A second point early determined by experiment and reflection was this: that the making or breaking of the circuit must be accomplished by the use of mercury, and not by a solid metallic connection. Various methods were tried, and soon abandoned as uncertain and irregular in their results; and the following plan was adopted:

"A small cross of delicate wire was mounted on a short axis of the same material, passing through the point of union of the four arms constituting the cross. This axis was then placed horizontal on a metallic support, in Y's, where it might vibrate, provided the top stem of the cross could be in some way attached to the pendulum of the clock, and the "cross" should thus rise and fall at its outer stem as the pendulum swings backward and forward. The metallic frame bearing the "cross" also bore a small glass tube bent at right angles. This was filled with mercury, and into one extremity one wire from the pole of the battery was made to dip; the other wire was made fast by a binding screw to the metallic stand bearing the "cross," and thus every time the "cross" dipped into the mercury in the bent tube, the electricity passed through the metallic frame, up the vertical standards bearing the axis of the cross, along the axis to the stem, and down the stem into the mercury, and finally through the mercury to the other pole of the battery. Thus at every swing of the pendulum the circuit was made, and a suitable apparatus might, by the electro-magnet, record each alternate second of time.

"The amount of power required of the pendulum to give motion to the delicate wire-cross was almost insensible, as the stems nearly counterpoised each other in every position. Here, however, there was great difficulty in procuring a fibre sufficiently minute and elastic to constitute the physical union between the top stem of the cross and the clock pendulum. Various materials were tried, among others a delicate human hair, the very finest that could be obtained, but this was too coarse and stiff. Its want of pliancy and elasticity gave to the minute "wire-cross" an irregular motion, and caused it to rebound from the globule of mercury into which it should have plunged. After many fruitless efforts, an appeal was made to an artisan of wonderful dexterity; the assistance of the *spider* was invoked; his web, perfectly elastic and perfectly pliable, was furnished, and this material connection between the wire-cross and the clock pendulum proved to be exactly the thing required. In proof of this remark I need only state the fact that one single spider's web has fulfilled the delicate duty of moving the wire-cross, lifting it, and again permitting it to dip into the mercury every second of time for a period of more than three years! How much longer it might have faithfully performed the same service I know not, as it then became necessary to break this admirable bond, to make some changes in the clock. Here it will be seen the same web was expanded and contracted each second during this whole period, and yet never, so far as could be observed, lost any portion of its elasticity. The clock was thus made to close the electric circuit in the most perfect manner; and inasmuch as the resistance opposed to the pendulum by the "wire-cross" was a constant quantity and very minute, thus acting precisely as does the resistance of the atmosphere, the clock, once regulated with the "cross" as a portion of its machinery, moved with its wonted steadiness and uniformity. Thus one grand point was gained. The clock was now ready to record its own beats automatically and with absolute certainty, without in any way affecting the regularity of its movement. It was early objected to the mercurial connection just described, that in a short time the surface of the mercury would become oxydized, and thus refuse to transmit the current of electricity; but experiment demonstrated that the explosion produced by the electric discharge at every dip into the mercury threw off the oxyd formed, and left the polished surface of the globule of mercury in a perfect state to receive the next passage of the electricity.

"So far as known, all other methods are now abandoned, and the mercurial connection is the only one in use.

"THE TIME-SCALE.—The clock being now prepared to record its beats, accurately and uniformly, the next important step was to obtain, if possible, a uniformly moving time-scale, which should be applicable to the practical demands of the astronomer

"In case the fillet of paper used in the Morse telegraph could have been made to flow at a uniform rate upon its surface, the clock could now record, its beats appearing as dots separated from each other by equal intervals. But it was soon seen that the paper could not be made to flow uniformly; and even had this been possible, a single night's work would demand for its record such a vast amount of paper that this method was inapplicable to practice. After careful deliberation, the 'revolving disk' was selected as the best possible surface on which the record of time and observation could be made. The preference was given to the disk over the cylinder for the following reasons: The uniform revolution of the disk could be more readily reached. The record on the disk was always under the eye in every part of it at the same time, while, on the revolving cylinder, a portion of the work was always invisible. One disk could be substituted for another with greater ease, and in a shorter time; and the measure of the fractions of seconds could be more rapidly and accurately performed on the disk than on the cylinder.

"After much thought and experiment it was decided to adopt 'a make circuit' and 'a dotted scale' rather than a 'break circuit' and a 'linear scale;' and I think it will be seen hereafter that in this selection the choice has been fully justified in practice. These points being settled, the mechanical problems now presented for solution were the following: First, To invent some machinery which could give to a disk of, say, twenty inches diameter, mounted on a vertical axis, a motion such that it should revolve uniformly once in each minute of time; and, second, To connect with this disk the machinery which should enable the clock to record on the disk each alternate second of time, in the shape of a delicate round dot. Third, The apparatus which should enable the observer to record on the same disk the exact moment of the transit of a star across the meridian, or the occurrence of any other phenomenon.

"The first of these problems was by far the most difficult, and, indeed, its perfect solution remains yet to be accomplished, though, for any practical astronomical purpose, the problem has been solved in more than one way.

"The plan adopted in the Cincinnati Observatory may be described as follows: The clock-work machinery employed to give to the great equatorial telescope a uniform motion equal to that of the earth's rotation, on its axis, offered to me the first obvious approximate solution of the problem under consideration. This machinery was accordingly applied to the motion of the disk, or rather to *regulate* the motion of revolution, this motion being produced by a descending weight, after the fashion of an ordinary clock. It was soon discovered that the 'Frauenhofer clock,' as this machine is called, was not competent to produce a motion of such uniformity as was now required. Several modifications were made with a positive gain; but after long study it was finally discovered that when the machinery was brought into perfect adjustment, the dynamical equilibrium obtained was an equilibrium of instability; that is, if from a motion such as produced a revolution in one exact minute, it began to lose, this loss or decrement in velocity went on increasing, or if it commenced to gain, the increment went on increasing at each revolution of the disk. Now all these delicate changes could be watched with the most perfect certainty; as, in case the disk revolved uniformly once a minute, then the seconds' dots would fall in such a manner (as we shall see directly) that the dots of the same recorded seconds would radiate from the center of the disk in a straight line. Any deviation from this line would be marked with the utmost delicacy down to the thousandth of a second. By long and careful study, it was at length discovered, that to make any change in the velocity of the disk, to increase or decrease quickly its motion, in short, to restore the dynamical equilibrium, the winding key of the 'Frauenhofer clock' was the point of the machinery where the extra helping force should be applied; and it was found that a person of ordinary intelligence, stationed at the disk, and with his fingers on this key, could, whenever he noticed a slight deviation from uniformity, at once, by slight assistance, restore the equilibrium, when the machine would perhaps continue its performance perfectly for several minutes, when again some slight acceleration or retardation might be required from the sentinel posted as an auxiliary.

"The mechanical problem now demanding solution was very clearly announced. It was this: Required to construct an automaton which should take the place of the intelligent sentinel, watch the going of the disk, and instantly correct any acceleration or retardation. This, in fact, is the great problem in all efforts to secure uniform motion of rotation. This problem was resolved theoretically, in many ways, several of which methods were executed mechanically without success, as it was found that the machine stationed as a sentinel to regulate the going of the disk was too weak, and was itself carried off by its too powerful antagonist. The following method was, however, in the end, entirely successful. Upon the axis of the winding key, already mentioned, a toothed wheel was attached, the gearing being so adjusted that one revolution of this wheel should produce a whole number of revolutions of the disk. The circumference of this wheel was cut into a certain number of notches, so that, as it revolved, one of these notches would reach the highest point once in two seconds of time. By means of an electro-magnet a small cylinder or roller, at the extremity of a lever arm, was made to fall into the highest notch of the toothed wheel at the end of every two seconds. In case the disk was revolving exactly once a minute, the roller, driven by the sidereal clock, by means of an electro-magnet, fell to the bottom of the notch, and performed no service whatever; but, in case the disk began to slacken its velocity, then the roller fell on the retreating inclined face of the notch, and thus urged forward by a minute amount the laggard disk, while, on the contrary, should the variation from a uniform velocity present itself in an acceleration, then the roller struck on the advancing face of the notch, and thus tended slowly to restore the equilibrium. Let it be remembered that this delicate regulator has but a minute amount of service to perform. It is ever on guard, and detecting, as it does instantly, any disposition to change, at once applies its restoring power, and thus preserves an exceedingly near approach to exact uniformity of revolution. This regulator operates through all the wheel-work, and thus accomplishes a restoration by minute increments or decrements spread over many minutes of time.

"With a uniformly revolving disk, stationary in position, we should accomplish exactly, and very perfectly, the record of one minute of time, presenting on the recording surface thirty dots at equal angular intervals on the circumference of a circle. To receive the *time dots* of the next minute on a circle of larger diameter, required either that the recording pen should change position, or that at the end of each revolution the disk itself should move away from the pen by a small amount. We chose to remove the disk. To accomplish accurately the change of position of the disk, at the end of each revolution, the entire machine was mounted on wheels on a small railway track, and by a very delicate mechanical arrangement accomplished its own change of position between the fifty-ninth and sixtieth second of every minute."

The foregoing explanations are given as a mere illustration of Professor Mitchel's mechanical ingenuity. To the great world he is better known by other and more striking characteristics.

As a *lecturer* Professor Mitchel had a remarkable

gift: his fervid oratory was natural; it was the truest exemplification of the trite but striking idea of the poet,

"Thoughts that breathe, and words that burn."

He could make a dry problem in mathematical astronomy so pleasing, by its clear and eloquent presentation, as to enchain a popular assembly and extort their applause both for problem and lecturer. His language, purely extemporaneous, was beautiful; his figures and illustrations strikingly well chosen; and his voice and manner powerful and overmastering. Sometimes his fervor seemed like a Delphian inspiration; and there are few who will forget the magnificent effects produced by his lectures on the Astronomy of the Bible, which are found in this volume. Those who heard him deliver them will easily recall the almost inspired speaker, and hear again in memory, the lectures as they read them.

As a true and whole-hearted *patriot* he had no superior. Influenced by this spirit, he tore himself from home ties, alas! not capable of bearing the rude parting,—his departure cost him his cherished wife; and thus he gave himself up to his country. All his energies, all his talents, his varied education, his fame, his brilliant future; whatever there was of power or influence in him or his name, was hers, devoted to her with a single eye and a single purpose. And he died for her, as truly, as devotedly,—shall we not say as gloriously,—as though he had fallen leading a forlorn hope to turn disaster into victory?

But as a *soldier* his whole-hearted patriotism was of great value. Bred at West Point, and having engrafted upon that thorough elementary education the knowledge of men, of life, of practical science and industrial arts, he was the very *beau-ideal* of a general. Full of resources, he made bridges of cotton-bales and fence-rails, and was the first man across to test their precarious structure. Restlessly energetic, his mind passed like lightning over every part of a plan or a field; his quick glance caught the capabilities of a position; his experience provided whatever was needed; his surplus vitality, overflowing his own person, swept out among the soldiers and put the whole mass in motion. His great personal bravery was a constant example and incentive to every man under his command. Wherever he appeared, there was work to do: expeditions, rapid movements, concerted combinations, forced marches. Without making too sweeping a remark, we may consider General Mitchel as among the very best of our commanders; and, had he lived, he would have risen to a position in public esteem and confidence second to none in the land.

As a devout Christian,—not presented now to the world in the mere statement of a charitable opinion, which gives "a good conscience" to every public man who dies,—but as a consistent, conscientious, devout Christian man, General Mitchel is best known to his home and his intimate friends. Admiring, as they do, his brilliant qualities; his learning, his genius, his military fame, they recur with far more comfort to the fact of his holy and fervent life, his daily communing with his God, his practical piety, his certain and holy hope of eternal life through the blood of Christ.

No king stood by his dying bed beseeching him—

> If thou think'st on Heaven's bliss,
> Hold up thy hand, make signal of thy hope."

Prompted by the unutterable thoughts which crowded upon him, he gave, unbidden, such a happy signal, literally holding up his hand, and pointing to that world beyond the skies, which was then lifting " its everlasting portals high" to greet him with an immortal radiance, such as even his enthusiastic astronomy had never conceived. His last words, brokenly uttered, were taken down by his aid-de-camp, and they add another to the ever-increasing and enduring testimonies, that, when the good man dies, God alone is great, and Heaven alone is real existence.

General Mitchel was, as might be expected, the recipient of many honors, due to his own merits. He had filled many offices and posts. A graduate of West Point, he was a lieutenant of artillery, a lawyer, a railway engineer, an astronomer; the founder of one observatory, the director of two; a Doctor of Laws from more than one institution; a Fellow of the Royal Astronomical Society, and of several other foreign societies; a Major-General of Volunteers. In 1841, he was a member of the Board of Visitors at the Military Academy. In 1847 and 1848 he was Adjutant-General of the State of Ohio. He was elected a member of the American Philosophical Society in 1853.

H. C.

UNIVERSITY OF PENNSYLVANIA,
PHILADELPHIA, *March*, 1862.

LECTURE I.

ASTRONOMICAL EVIDENCES OF THE BEING OF A GOD.

LECTURE I.

ASTRONOMICAL EVIDENCES OF THE BEING OF GOD.

THE topics upon the discussion of which I am about to venture, are far different from those which have hitherto engaged our attention. We are no longer to follow the career of the human mind, in its efforts to trace the laws of the physical universe. We stand with the philosopher and astronomer on the very apex of that stupendous pyramid, which human genius has reared by the protracted labor of six thousand years. We are lifted far above the clouds of earth. An interminable vista, broad as the universe, illimitable as space, teeming with myriads of flaming orbs, rises up to meet our vision. We have attained to a knowledge of the potent laws which extend their dominion over these countless millions. We are permitted to examine the

"Thrones, dominations, princedoms, virtues, powers,"

which fill the heavens. Our view sweeps from

the humble satellite which acknowledges and obeys the superior power of the earth, through systems, and schemes, and universes, whose vastness no stretch of thought can comprehend, whose numbers no arithmetic of earth can count. We no longer seek to weigh these ponderous orbs, we seek not to trace their wanderings, we attempt not to compute their reciprocal influences or to predict their cycles of configuration or their mighty periods of revolution. We shall attempt to rise far beyond and above all these inquiries, and venture on the far more difficult task of reasoning our way through these wonderful displays of wisdom and power, to the ultimate source of all wisdom and power.

We shall venture to inquire whence has sprung the Physical Universe? what hand has launched these flaming orbs in space? Whose eye omniscient has traced out their untrodden paths? what hand omnipotent upholds the stupendous fabric of Nature?

These are themes of superlative grandeur. No mind can approach their contemplation without an expansion of thought, an uplifting of the powers of the soul, a sensation resembling that which swept across the soul of our great ancestor, when it was whispered, "Ye shall be as gods;" and there comes a withering sense of our own weakness, a consciousness of our utter inability to scale these lofty heights, or penetrate the deep profound which stretches out before us. If called upon to discuss these themes in the presence of superior beings, the Hierarchs of Heaven, resplendent with exalted wisdom, it would be utter folly to unseal the lip, or move the tongue to the utterance of one solitary thought.

But I address not myself to angelic intelligences, but to man, humble, trusting, inquiring, teachable man, conscious of his own weakness, and ever ready to receive with feelings of charitable consideration, the humble efforts of those, who, like himself, are struggling to discover truth.

I have ventured then to propound for examination the following train of investigation:—*Does the Physical Universe proclaim the Being of a God?* Should this inquiry be affirmatively answered, we propose to inquire, *If the God thus revealed, is the same august and eternal being portrayed in our sacred books.* I shall then consider these sacred books in their relation to the determinate truths of science, to compare their revelations of the cosmogony of the universe with the revelations of modern science, to examine critically the astronomical illustrations, allusions, and miracles of the historians, poets, and prophets of the sacred volume, and finally to compare the Hebrew chronology with that of the primitive nations of the earth. Such is the train of investigation to which I would lead your thoughts, humbly premising in the outset, that I have most earnestly desired, that this task might devolve on some one far abler than myself to effect its almost impossible execution.

If we examine the globe we inhabit with any degree of attention, we perceive its mighty surface, diversified with mountain and plain, with ocean and forest, and teeming with animal and vegetable life. Its exterior surrounded with an atmospheric envelope of subtle character, in which and by which all life is sustained, and without which universal death would reign upon the entire surface of the earth.

We find our globe accompanied in its flight through space by another of smaller dimensions, and that each is related to the other by bonds which are never severed. These associated worlds are in their turn linked to a vast central orb, from which they derive their light, and heat, and life. Conjoined with these, and linked to the same grand center, we behold a great multitude of orbs, vast in their proportions, diverse in form, differing in mass, all however obedient to one all-pervading law, and all moving, with the most astonishing harmony, within the regions of space prescribed by this all-prevalent law. Lifting our eyes above this mighty scheme of revolving worlds, we behold the starry Heavens. Each glittering point is doubtless but a repetition of the system with which we are specifically allied. These by aggregations again form grander schemes, clusterings of suns and systems, peopling the boundless regions of space, ranging in wonderful and overwhelming prospective, as far as human vision aided by the most powerful optic aid can penetrate the deep domain of ether. Throughout this boundless universe we perceive that the most perfect harmony prevails— each one of the countless myriads of worlds, moving with swift velocity in its appointed circuit, swaying and being swayed, but ever keeping its appointed orbit, and performing with strict precision its admirable revolution. There is no confusion, no jarring of contending worlds, no collisions of flying orbs to disturb the harmony of Heaven.

Such is the celestial mechanism, admirable in its perfection, boundless in its dimensions, overwhelming in its diversity, countless in its myriads of parts, and yet one mighty unit, for whose structure and being we are called upon to account.

The human mind has thus far framed but three hypotheses, to resolve the enigma of this stupendous universe :—

1. It has been conceived that the universe is eternal, without beginning and without end; passing through cycles of change, but returning into itself, like the ceaseless revolutions of the planetary orbs.

2. A second hypothesis demands the eternity of matter, and attributes the laws of the universe and its existent organization to blind fate or chance, resting its perpetuity on the same uncertain foundation.

3. A third hypothesis ascribes the existent universe to the creation of an Eternal Mind, omnipotent, omniscient, filling with his presence the universe, and upholding all things at every instant by his Almighty will.

These three hypotheses now demand our careful philosophic and unprejudiced examination. Let no one be startled at the boldness of this discussion. Truth is mighty and must prevail.

We commence then with the first hypothesis. It is asserted by some that the universe is eternal, that the same sun which now vivifies the earth has ever poured upon it its flood of light, that the same moon which now sways the ocean tide, has ever circled round the earth, that the same heavens which now blaze upon the sight, have ever shone with the same effulgence, and shall ever shine throughout the ceaseless ages of eternity. That the generations of earth perish, and are reproduced, and have been ever perishing and being reproduced from all eternity. In the examination of this hypothesis, there comes to us but little light from the surrounding orbs of the universe. It would be difficult to prove that these silent and mysterious worlds, now sweeping through the trackless regions of space, ever did commence their wonderful career. We are rather restricted to an examination of that planet which we inhabit, and our reasoning with reference to its physical being and constitution, may by analogy be safely transferred to more distant worlds. If the hypothesis in question be true, it must account for every phenomenon of nature. If it assert that the world is eternal, then it must in like manner assert, that all upon its surface is eternal in its series, perishing indeed, but being reproduced in an endless series. Were it then possible to penetrate the inmost recesses of the earth, and to read the history of the ages which are past, in case any traces remain of what once was, we might anticipate finding the memorials of generations sweeping backward indefinitely into the womb of time. If the earth be eternal, then is its physical constitution eternal; its animal and vegetable life eternal in series, and man in his generations, must in like manner be pronounced eternal. In the decision of these fundamental questions, we are not left to mere conjecture. It may be asserted that the planets are eternal, and reason may fail to disprove the bold assertion, but science has read, with keen and penetrating glance, the past history of the revolutions of the surface of our globe. Go to the naturalist and the geologist, and they will unfold to you the rocky leaves of the earth's primeval history. They will carry you backward by slow degrees, through a vast series of vegetable and animal existence, until a point is reached, in this grand investigation, where science plants her foot on the primitive rock and declares, that here is an existence anterior to every form of animal or vegetable life. This planet indeed then existed, but on its surface surged a boundless, interminable ocean, without shore, without life. Here, then, we reach a most wonderful era. After the deposition of these primitive rocks, came a series of phenomena, more startling and stupendous than even the generation of the orbs of Heaven. Life, that mystery of mysteries, bursts upon the universe. It, we know, does not sweep down upon us from out the mists which shroud in gloom the eternity of the past. Life is the offspring of time. In the fullness of time, the tender plant, the drooping flower, a teeming vegetation, burst upon the world. These are not eternal; backward we trace their sources from age to age remote, until we stand at a point anterior to all such existence, and pronounce unhesitatingly, here is the beginning. If this be true of vegetable life, it is more emphatically true of animal existence. This too in all its classes, orders, species, and generations is the offspring of time. Deeply bound in the solid rocks of earth, we trace its existence from age to age, until the series is exhausted and we again pronounce, here is the beginning; at this point sentient being first inhaled the breath of life; at this point the eye first beheld the beauties of primeval nature, and the appetite first sought to satisfy its cravings from the luxuriant bosom of the mother of all life. Once more we pronounce positively, that man is the offspring of time. Individually ephemeral, even in his generations he can not assert the smallest claim to an eternity past.

A few thousand years of his history and of that of the race is on record. During this minute portion of time, we are able to trace with positive distinctness, the rapid and unequivocal advances of the race in power, in knowledge, in wisdom. During this brief period, man's empire over nature and nature's exhaustless powers and resources, has been advancing with the most rapid strides. If, then, we are to judge from these facts, of the origin of our race, if the convergence of two lines determines with certainty their point of intersection, we are forced to admit either that the human race is of comparatively recent origin, or that it is only within the last few thousand years that we have attained to the power of advancing in wisdom, and in power.

No, matter, however, where or in what point we place the beginning of our race, this beginning falls in time, and posterior to every other form of life which marks the surface of our globe.

But all life is linked indissolubly with the physical constitution of the earth. The atmosphere is as much a portion of the planet, as the solid parts. This atmosphere is the vital fluid on which all animated nature depends. Sweep this covering from the earth, and universal death sways his empire over all things.

Again, life depends on organic condition, and the productions of earth give life to the myriads which inhabit her surface. Strike these laws of vivified production from existence, and all animated nature dies. But life is linked, in like manner, to the sun. Shut out his beams, the source of all heat and motion, and life soon languishes; decay, darkness, and death are again triumphant.

Thus it will be seen that even in the order of nature, as exhibited in one single dependent world, it is utterly impossible to assert an eternity of being, or an endless and interminable succession of events. Man is not eternal, animal life is not eternal, vegetable existence is not eternal. These all had a beginning, and we are driven from our first hypothesis, and forced to admit that it does not account for the existent phenomena of the Physical Universe.

We now reach the consideration of the second hypothesis. This asserts that the matter of the Physical Universe is eternal, and that the existent organization, in all its interminable ramifications, of world, and sun, and system, in all its varieties of life, and being, and organic existence, is attributable to *fate* or *chance*. It is, perhaps, impossible to demonstrate, or to disprove directly, the eternity of matter. The mind does seemingly comprehend the idea of the eternity of space, and were matter unorganized it might be quite possible to conceive of the eternity of matter. We shall, therefore, examine in the outset, the last assertion of this hypothesis; that the existent order of universe being is the offspring of chance, or accident.

We have already asserted that the organization of the universe is exceedingly complex, although subjected to the action of one universal law. No one body in space is isolated or independent. Each and every one is linked to all others, and a reciprocal influence is exerted through the boundless regions of space. Even the subordinate organizations are complex. Take for example the system of planets and satellites dependent on our sun. Here is a celestial mechanism of astonishing complexity, yet of admirable order and beauty. Examine for a moment the multitude of concurring accidents, required to produce one such system, and to hold it steady in all the innumerable configurations of its revolving orbs. We call on accident or chance to account for the selection of the law of universal gravitation, of the laws of motion, of the figures of the planets, of the direction of their motions, of the courses of their orbits, of their relative positions, of their relative masses, of their relative distances. We call on chance to adapt the physical constitution of our globe, to the sustentation of animal and vegetable life. We are obliged to demand of chance, the structure of the human frame, and all its multiplied adaptations to the circumstances by which it is surrounded. But this is all demanded in one single system. But we rise still higher to the contemplation of double and multiple suns, and yet higher to the stable organization of mighty clusters of stars, all brought into being by chance, and accidentally arranged for an ever-during perpetuity. If those who advocate the doctrine of chance are governed by its laws, the improbability accumulates on their hands, as we rise higher and higher, until it amounts almost if not quite, to an infinite improbability, against this hypothesis of accident.

In case we apply this doctrine of chance to the investigation of one of the simplest problems which it is required to resolve, we shall become convinced of its utter incapacity to account for the complicated phenomena of nature. Let us admit, for the sake of the argument, that by chance the orbs of heaven were formed, by chance they assumed their present figure, by chance they came to attract each other, according to the inverse square of their distances, by chance the subordinate planets are hurled into space, by chance these planets select their present beautiful orbits, by chance these orbits are so located as to exclude the possibility of interference, by chance, in short, all the subordinate organizations are completed around the innumerable suns, which now, by chance, fill the capacious domains of space. All this is admitted, and now we demand of this same chance, to account for the present distribution of these stars of heaven. Are the aggregations and configurations now existent the result of accident, or does mathematical demonstration show them to be grouped by some power rising superior to accident, and swaying an influence even beyond the empire of chance?

Even in this narrow, contracted domain of accident, the profoundest investigations have banished this imaginary monster being from his empire, and the demonstration is clear and positive, that even in comparatively simple aggregations of stars, these groupings can not be the effect of accident, but must be the result of some superior overruling law or power. The universe is not, then, an accidental arrangement of matter. Reason forbids the adoption of such an hypothesis in the face of millions of chances to one against the possibility of such an organization even in one of its humblest departments. There seems, therefore, but one remaining hypothesis for examination. If the mind can not reach to certainty, can not find a resting-place in the belief of an eternal, an omniscient Creator, it is vain to hope that there ever can be found a solid resting-place for the doubts which toss the human mind to and fro on a stormy sea of speculation.

To this last hypothesis, then, we gladly invite your attention—the most sublime, the most comprehensive, the most dignified and far-reaching of the three. By it we are lifted out of the domain of darkness, from the dominion of fatality, and, in case it can be demonstrated, our feet are set upon an eternal rock. What, then, does this third hypothesis affirm? It affirms that the existent universe, in all its diversified and multitudinous parts, is an effect dependent upon, and deriving its being from, a great first cause. That this cause is eternal, preëxistent, sentient, and omnipotent, competent to call into being the universe of matter, to endow this created matter with certain qualities and properties, to select with wisdom from among an infinity of laws those alone adequate to the government of a universe, with power to enforce eternally the administration of these laws over the organisms either derived from the operation of these laws, or dependent for existence upon their pervading influence. In short, this hypothesis asserts that this primeval cause is an infinite and eternal order-loving, ever-active God. Such, then, is the amazing proposition we are called upon to discuss; and may that Power, to the recognition of whose existence our feeble reasonings have led us, give to us the strength to lift your minds, in like manner, upward through Nature to Nature's God!

Let us, then, if it be possible, permit our imaginations to wander backward through the silent ages of the past, until we reach an epoch so remote that we stand in the midst of untenanted space. The wide universe is nothing but unbounded, limitless vacuity. There is room for a universe, but as yet no particle of the myriads which are to people space have any existence. And now conceive, if you can, of the generation of the first particle of matter; there it is in the midst of darkness unfathomable, surrounded by boundless vacuity. Left to itself what is to become of this solitary particle? Shall it remain forever fixed, immoveable in the same absolute point of space? Shall it move when there is no motion? Shall it sink when there is neither height nor depth? Whither shall it go? Or left to itself, what mind can conceive the destiny of this primeval atom of infinity? Here it would seem that in the very outset, in the very birth of matter, mind is imperiously demanded to endue matter with the attributes of existence. Look at this inert, lifeless, senseless, motionless particle of matter; surround it by myriads on myriads as dull and insensate as itself, and how utterly inconsistent is it, with all the attributes of reason, to conceive that such a mass can of itself give to itself qualities and properties; select for itself laws of organization and being; construct itself into complex schemes, and flying worlds, and wondrous systems; fill these worlds with life, and light, and beauty; and above all, people them with intelligences, capable of penetrating the profound mysteries of the universe, and of scanning the most complex organisms which fill the regions of space. We are forced away from such an absurdity: against it reason rebels. Matter, then, has no power. In vain do we seek within it for the secret of its existence. To the inquiry, Whence come its attributes? it yields no response, because it has no response to yield. But grant, if you please, its chaotic existence— scatter it profusely, as far as thought can penetrate the deep profounds—leave it without the sustaining hand of Omnific power,—and no thought can fathom the future of a universe thus filled. If there be powers of segregation and aggregation among the existent particles (an impossible supposition), then why may not these particles, fitted for the organization of man, flying from the four quarters of the universe, seek each other, build up the solid bones, knit the tough muscle, inflate with life's purple current the vein and artery, mould into symmetry the wondrous form, and fashion man in the very womb of chaos wild, in the midst of darkness profound, surrounded by forms wilder than imagination has ever pictured? The mind revolts from such a supposition, and exclaims, Strike from existence this insensate matter, these germs of Being, or place them under the controlling power of wisdom supreme.

In vain, then, do we seek any organization, however defective, without a God. We wander in darkness infinite; not a beam of light illumines the gloom of eternal night. The mind labors and struggles to rise, but plumes its wing in vain, and beats vacuity as it struggles downward to a still darker deep. These, then, are some of the negative evidences of the Being of God.

Let us now examine more closely the existent celestial mechanism, and from it learn its positive teachings on this most important subject. If supreme intelligence have superintended the organization of the universe, then will the evidences of this august power be stamped on every part and portion of the celestial organisms. Even here on earth, within the range of the dominion governed by the intelligence of the human mind, how infallibly do we pass from the effect to the cause, from the thing fashioned to the framer, from the design to the higher intelligence which planned and executed the design. Who has ever stood within the portals of the lofty St. Peter's, that majestic temple of the living God, and gazed upon its vast proportions, its mighty columns, its interminable arches, its viewless dome, rising grand, majestic, and overwhelming; who I say has gazed upon those wonders of art, without reverting to the god-like mind that conceived this stupendous fabric, and fashioned its vast proportions in beauty and in strength? Mind is there radiant in every form, pervading every curve of beauty, beaming from every shape of strength and perpetuity. If in this earthly structure, this beautiful atom on the broad bosom of our mother earth, we discern that which bespeaks the immortality of mind, what doth the solid earth itself declare,—radiant with power and beauty, teeming with life, and not life's images, verdant with beauty, diversified with every variety of grandeur, rolling ever on its firm axle, irradiated with a flood of splendor and alternately canopied with jeweled glories, sweeping onward freighted with its nine hundred millions of intelligent beings, its myriads of sentient creatures, circling for ever in its appointed path. Spring-time and harvest, summer and winter do never fail. There is bread for the eater, and seed for the sower. Poise yourself in empty space and behold this revolving world, with its rocks and mountains, its forests and oceans, its life and energy sweeping by you, swiftly revolving, and swiftly flying, growing, swelling, expanding, as it approaches, till as it flashes by you, the imagination is overwhelmed with the amazing grandeur!

Is there here no evidence of mind? whose hand fashioned this stupendous globe, and filled its mighty cavities with the heaving deep? who painted with glowing tints its limitless expanse; warmed, and vivified, and fructified its teeming bosom; filled its surface with life and energy, with hope, and love, and happiness; launched it flaming through the abyss of space, firm fixed in its appointed course as though linked by chains of adamant, never, never to be moved? The swelling mind answers, "It is God, it is God alone!"

But this is mere external examination. Let us penetrate still deeper into the arcana of this wonderful exhibition, and mark the admirable adaptation of all its parts. Living, sentient intelligence, seems to be the grand aim of the mighty architect;—the sustentation of man, the monarch of creation. For him the earth teems with fruit and flower, with the rich harvest and the golden grain. For him the fresh fountains leap from the solid rock, and the cattle feed on a thousand hills. To lull him to repose the solid earth turns away from the too brilliant sun, and the gentle stars light the nocturnal sky. To wake him to vigor, the morning dawns and the light of day, tempered by a provision of admirable efficiency, swells gently into brighter and still brighter effulgence, until the full-orbed sun bursts in splendor upon the world.

How and by what wonderful contrivance are all these results accomplished? The life of man is dependent on the purity of the wonderful envelope which surrounds the earth. Sweep away this gauzy atmosphere and he dies, and with him all life becomes extinct. Even permit this atmosphere to stagnate, and pestilence fills the earth. But how shall this gaseous ocean be heaved from its mighty depths? who shall fan the breeze, or stir the wind, or rouse the sweeping tornado? Look at yonder distant fiery globe, ninety-five millions of miles removed from our earth, and who would suppose that from this distant orb, comes the mysterious power by which this mighty aerial ocean, the breath of life to man, to animal, and to vegetable, is stirred to its profoundest depths, and its purification wrought out by laws and influences of the most intricate character.

And yet the sun is "the prince of the power of the air." By his heat operating through the laws of expansion and contraction, mobility becomes the attribute of every atmospheric particle — change, circulation, ceaseless motion, sometimes revealing itself in the gentle zephyr that plays with the drooping floweret, and anon mightily, in the fierce tempest which wrestles with the gnarled oak.

Not only is the remote but powerful sun the "prince of the power of the air," but from his bosom emanates that yet more mysterious influence which heaves up from the broad ocean those vast vaporous masses, which, swiftly borne on the chariot of the bird, sweep over the surface of the earth, distilling in gentle dews, or bursting forth in the fierce deluge.

Here, then, are most astonishing adaptations —the sun, the earth, the ocean, the atmosphere, the laws of heat, of motion, of expansion, of evaporation, of condensation—all combining to work out the most beneficent influences for man, the sole recipient of the blessings which flow from the harmonious on-going of this complex, but never-failing mechanism. Wonderful contrivance! by whose power and influence the earth teems with the rich harvest and the ripened corn invites the sickle of the reaper. To perfect all this astonishing development, an adequate supply of moisture is demanded, an adequate supply of light is demanded, an adequate supply of heat is demanded; certain qualities of soil are demanded, and above all, the fecundity of nature is demanded. Whence do all these come? Whence these admirable means to an end? The power of human genius may collect together the material from the four quarters of the earth, and compound a fruitful soil, the same genius may supply the required irrigation, but what stretch of human power, can supply the needed heat, or bid the dead seed burst into life?

A further examination shows the nicest and most astonishing adjustments. In case the annual supply of heat were increased or diminished by even a single degree, the most disastrous consequences would follow. An increase or decrease of thrice this quantity would destroy every form of life, which now fills the earth. That this annual supply may be constant, look at the wonderful complexity of contrivance. The great center, the mighty reservoir of light and heat, is made exhaustless; pouring for ever from its bosom a flood of light and heat, borne in the most inscrutable manner athwart the regions of space, with a velocity overwhelming. Thousands of years has the light blazed, and splendor undimmed; and the heat flashed with power undiminished. The source, then, is constant, though ever exhausting. But this is not the only requisite. The earth, the recipient of these beams of heat and light, must turn its various faces to the source of life—and here another wonder breaks upon us. This solid globe, with a diameter of 8000 miles, with unchanged continuity of motion, is ever turning on its well-poised axle. The conditions of perfection require an absolute uniformity in the motion of rotation. Any thing short of this would derange the economy of nature, and mar the perfection of the plan. Amid the conflicting causes tending to destroy or derange the uniformity of rotation, an admirable equilibrium is evolved, and so long as time shall endure, day and night shall not fail in their season. In this particular the earth is freed from the effects of all external power, subjected alone to the action of that primitive impulse which set it spinning on its never changing axle.

While uniformity of rotation is an essential element; the equal and perfect distribution of light and heat, it is not the only one: a still more complex and difficult guarantee is required. The earth, in its orbitual movement around the sun, must cling to the primitive figure of its annual orbit. Slight changes are indeed admissible, but the limits are narrow, and the wonder is how may change exist at all without derangement fatal to the complex scheme. Here we find a multitude of disturbing forces. The moon, powerful by her proximity, sways the solid earth: the interior planets, Mercury and Venus, in like manner exert their influence: the larger planets, Jupiter and Saturn, claim their share in this perpetual struggle; the smaller planets, the remote satellites, even the shadowy comets assert their power, and the earth is dragged by contending forces in every possible direction. Yet are all these contending powers so admirably equipoised, the one against the other, that this mighty globe flies through space, acknowledging in her every movement the effects of all these differing causes, yet ever linked to her orbit, slowly changing, but never changed.

Thus do we see how wonderfully the various

parts of this diversified scheme are knit together. Not a blade of grass, or a delicate flower shoots into life, that is not dependent on the entire organization of the vast scheme of planetary worlds, which sweep in concord around their common center. Does not all this perfection of plan, infinitely ramified and diversified, beautiful, perfect, admirable, ever perpetuated, not a link (however small) wanting in the infinite net-work, spreading through every kingdom of nature, rising to embrace the sun itself and its attendant planets,—does not all this mighty display of contrivance demonstrate with irresistible power the being of a God?

If we lift our thoughts above our earth and survey the various worlds which revolve about our sun, the same evidence of design meets us at every point. Our earth is one of the humblest of all the planets. If we visit the mighty system of Jupiter, such is the vastness of its celestial architecture that all we have left behind appears trivial and insignificant. If we go yet further, and survey the still more amazing system of Saturn, with its retinue of attending moons, and its girdle of enigmatical rings of light, we find displays of power and wisdom so resistless, that if all other worlds were stricken from existence, enough would here remain to demonstrate the being of a God. But these are not separate existences. They are not quiescent orbs fixed on some unimaginable foundation in space. They are all indissolubly united, and all flying through space. Whence, then, come the wonderful laws of their reciprocal influence, and whence the laws which curb their high career? These laws of reciprocal action and of motion are the only ones, under whose dominion the planetary scheme could exist. Relax for a single moment the continuity of their power, and chaos instantly engulfs the fair fabric of creation. Relax only the power of gravitation and every planet shoots madly from its orbit; augment ever so slightly its power, the equilibrium is destroyed, and world after world sinks into the sun. If in the revolution of countless ages, all possible laws have by chance held their sway, and the present laws have been upturned in the long range of possibilities, then we demand how comes it that they endure? Why do they not give place to other schemes in their turn? This we know is not the fact. For more than three thousand years in the past history of our system, there has been no shadow of change in these mighty laws of nature, — unyielding in themselves, steadily have they wrought out their legitimate results. Now what are these laws? Are they attributes of inert matter? This is impossible. Go to the chemist, bid him apply the most powerful tests, the most subtle analysis, and exhaust his powers of research, and then let him answer if he have found the essence of gravitation. In vain do we seek for these alternates: we are forced again to take refuge in our great hypothesis, and to declare that these so called laws of nature are but the uniform expression of the will of an ever-living God.

The uniformity and perpetuity of these laws alone furnish the opportunity for human intelligence to rise through their examination, in their multitudinous effects, upward to the great source of all law. Were their action capricious or uncertain, no power of genius could have reached to a knowledge of their existence, and darkness would have ever shrouded the human mind.

If we extend our researches beyond the limits of the solar system, and, passing across the mighty gulf which separates us from the starry heavens, inspect minutely the organizations which are there displayed, we find the dominion of these same laws extending to these remote regions, and holding an imperious sway over revolving suns. Thus we perceive, that in one most important particular, the objects which compose the mighty universe are obviously alike, and seem to have sprung from a common origin. We are, moreover, compelled to admit a sun in every visible star; and if a sun, then attendant planets; and if revolving planets, then, likewise, some scheme of sentient existence, possibly remotely analogous to that which is displayed with such wonderful minuteness in our globe. Thus if the being of a God can be argued from the admirable adaptations which surround man in this nether world, every star that glitters in the vast concave of heaven proclaims, with equal power, this mighty truth. If we rise still higher, and from the contemplation of individual stars, examine their distribution, their clusterings, their aggregations into immense systems, the fact of their mutual influences, their restless and eternal activity, their amazing periods of revolution, their countless millions, and their ever-during organizations, the mind, whelmed with the display of grandeur, exclaims involuntarily, "This is the empire of a God!"

And now, how is the knowledge of this vast surrounding universe revealed to the mind of man? Here is, perhaps, the crowning wonder. Through the agency of light, a subtle, intangible, imponderable something, originating, apparently, in the stars and suns, darting with incredible velocity from one quarter of the universe to the other, whether in absolute particles of matter shot off from luminous bodies, or by traces of an ethereal fluid, who shall tell? This incomprehensible fluid falls upon an instrument of most insignificant dimensions, yet of most wonderful construction, the human eye, and, lo! to the mind what wonders start into being. Pictures of the most extravagant beauty cover the earth;

clouds dipped in the hues of heaven fill the atmosphere; the sun, the moon, the planets, come up from out of the deeps of space, and far more amazing still, the distant orbs of heaven, in their relative magnitudes, distances and motions, are revealed to the bewildered mind. We have only to proceed one step further, and bringing to the aid of the human eye, the auxiliary power of the optic glass, the mind is brought into physical association with objects which inhabit the confines of penetrable space. We take cognizance of objects so remote, that even the flashing element of light itself, by which they are revealed, flies on its errand ten times ten thousand years to accomplish its stupendous journey.

Strike the human eye from existence, and at a single blow, the sun is blotted out, the planets fade, the heavens are covered with the blackness of darkness, the vast universe shrinks to a narrow compass bounded by the sense of touch alone.

Such, then, is the organization of the universe, and such the means by which we are permitted to take cognizance of its existence and phenomena. If the feeble mind of man has achieved victories in the natural world—if his puny structures, which have survived the attacks of a few thousand years, proclaim the superiority of the intelligence of his mind to insensate matter—if the contemplation of the works of art and the triumphs of human genius, swells us into admiration at the power of this invisible spirit that dwells in mortal form,—what shall be the emotions excited, the ideas inspired, by the contemplation of the boundless universe of God?

LECTURE II.

THE GOD OF THE UNIVERSE IS JEHOVAH.

LECTURE II.

THE GOD OF THE UNIVERSE IS JEHOVAH.

THE sacred Scriptures teach us, in the most unequivocal language, the unity of God, the majesty and grandeur of his kingdom. Jehovah inhabiteth eternity, and filleth immensity by his presence. By his word the worlds were made, and by his power he upholdeth all things. Omnipotent, omniscient, omnipresent, he is "God over all, blessed for ever."

Such is the language of revelation,—such the truths taught by our sacred volume. If these are the declarations of God himself—and the same Almighty Being has built the physical universe—the revelations of science must accord with those of Scripture, and we shall find the attributes of God stamped in characters indelible on the workmanship of his hands.

Does the material universe declare the unity of God? Is the domain of nature divided or divisible? Is there evidence, in the building of the mighty fabric of the universe, that it has been planned and executed by one mind and by one hand?

The development of our knowledge of the material heavens, has been progressive from century to century. The deeper the human mind has penetrated into the arcana of nature, the more positive does the evidence become, with reference to its origin and government. In the primitive ages of the world, while yet the light of science had scarcely dawned upon the human intellect, when the heavens were a maze of wonder, and their golden hieroglyphs a mystery and a marvel, human genius could not have risen through this unknown empire, up to the knowledge of the attributes of God. Whatever deductions we may now reach in our researches, no one will venture for one moment to assert that the sacred writers, by the same means, reached to their notions of the being and attributes of God.

If we examine the system which surrounds the sun, we find a multitude of worlds, possessing general characteristics. They are generally globular, they are in motion, they describe orbits of specific forms allied to each other, they are all powerfully influenced by the sun, and they materially affect each other. The matter, then, which constitutes these worlds and the sun itself, seems to be identical in one of its great characteristics. When the capacious intellect of Newton reached the grand conclusion, that one law swayed its dominion over planet, and satellite, and comet,—when he demonstrated that the most solid and the most evanescent bodies were obedient to the great principle of attraction,—by a generalization as sublime as it was daring, he rose to the declaration, that every particle of matter in the universe attracted every other particle, by a power which diminished as the square of the distances between the particles increased. Here, then, is a statement which, if it be true, demonstrates, in the most positive manner, that the matter of which the worlds are built is identical in character. But again, the laws which govern moving bodies on earth are extended to those which inhabit space; and when the watchings of a thousand years had revealed the universality of the application of these laws to the worlds which constitute the cortège of the sun, the same bold generalization carried these same laws to the fixed stars, and attempted to fasten their dominion on every particle of matter. It will be seen at once that these mighty propositions are far from being self-evident. Their demonstration is the reward of long centuries of ardent, and earnest, and patient investigation. These laws were first fastened on the moon; next the planets, slowly, and one by one, in their near proximity to the sun, and, also, in their vast orbits deep buried in space, yielded to the empire of these potent laws; and, finally, the mysterious comet, aerial, chaotic, capricious in its eccentric career, was demonstrated to yield to the same potent sway.

This was, doubtless, a grand achievement thus to prove, that in one great scheme of associated worlds there was unity of design, unity in matter, and unity in law. But this system, vast as it is, embracing within its domain a sweep of no less than ten thousand millions of miles, is but an infinitesimal portion of the universe of God. Is it possible to reach to the starry heavens, passing the gulf of space which separates us from these far-distant worlds, and fasten the same laws which rule in our system, upon the myriads of orbs which crowd the domain of space? It is only within a few years that this great achievement has been accomplished. Among the stars some have been found in such near proximity, that their true character is only revealed by the most powerful telescopes. While to the unaided eye, and, indeed, in inferior instruments, they appear as single stars, a higher power discovers them to consist of two individual objects, in such close proximity of position, that their mingled rays are only to be divided by the most potent optical aid.

These objects, within the last half century, have attracted the attention of eminent philosophers, and the most astonishing phenomena have been revealed. These double suns have been seen to move—they are known to revolve; and the laws of their motion and revolution are identical with those which govern the planetary orbs which sweep round the sun. There is no deception here. Their orbits have been computed, their periods and places predicted on the hypothesis that the laws of motion and gravitation extended their empire over these starry worlds, and in every particular have these bold predictions been verified. How deeply, then, has science penetrated the dominion of these laws of nature! The distance is not to be measured by the unit employed in the survey of the sun's domain. In one instance, in which science has figured the orbits, prophesied the periods, weighed the masses, measured the distance of two associated suns, their distance from earth is such that their light, flying at the rate of twelve millions of miles in each minute, reaches us only after a journey of ten years. This is not a solitary instance. Many of a like character have been thoroughly investigated, and with like results.

We may affirm, then, with safety and certainty, that the countless millions of orbs which constitute the universe, are all fashioned from the same material, and are all in subjection to the dominion of the laws of motion and gravitation. As the scheme is one, as the matter is one, as the laws are the same, so one mind hath conceived the infinite plan, and one hand hath wrought out the magnificence of creation.

But the Scriptures disclose the *Omnipotence*, of God; he hath created all things by his wisdom, and by the might of his power. To the mind which fully comprehends the structure of the heavens, the power of the Almighty architect is most signally displayed: a superficial examination may not thus impress us. We witness from month to month the revolution of the moon about the earth, and from year to year their conjoined revolution about the sun; we trace the planets in their harmonious career; all is so simple, so beautiful, that the idea of the display of vast power does not at first come down upon the mind.

But let us for one moment contemplate, at nearer distance, these ponderous orbs. Examine, if you please our own earth, one of the smallest of them, and you find a solid globe of 8000 miles in diameter, possessing a weight so enormous, that any and all the structures of men upon its surface, sink to utter insignificance in the comparison, and weigh as the small dust of the balance. And yet, go to the Pyramids of Egypt, and contemplate those heavy relics of antiquity: how do their vast proportions, the solid rocks which constitute their mass, elevate our ideas of the power which reared these huge fabrics. But these are stationary. Could they be hurled with swift velocity, from their solid bases, by some mighty catapult, into space, never again to revisit the earth, our ideas of the power requisite to such a phenomenon would be greatly enlarged. Man, by superior wisdom, and by the exercise of that intellect which God has given, has gained a certain mastery over the potent forces of nature; hence, we witness with amazement, the fiery trains, which, with incredible velocity, fly upon the iron ways built for their appointed tracks. What stupendous power is developed in this fiery car of earth! We involuntarily shrink from its approach, and tremble as it dashes by us, flying with a speed of sixty miles in a single hour of time. But what are these atoms compared with the solid earth itself, and what the display of power here, when compared with that which launched this mighty globe, with its continents and oceans, into space, and hath dashed it with a velocity such that its hourly journey is sixty-eight thousand miles? Or look yet higher to God's fiery car, the sun, linked to a thousand revolving worlds! onward its mighty mass, a million of miles in diameter, sweeps through space, bearing with it its retinue of flaming worlds.

God's mighty arm hath projected these stupendous orbs, and his omnipotent power alone hath impressed upon them their amazing velocity. It is not possible to escape from this conclusion, by arguing the laws of motion and attraction. These are but the modes in which God exercises his power, they are not the power itself. Let some gigantic arm reach out and attempt to arrest the moon; were the trial possible, were the power of every human arm concentrated into one, even the power of the thousands of generations which have peopled the earth, even this combined and concentrated power could not check this puny orb of heaven for one single moment in its swift career.

Again, what mighty force restrains the planets in their orbits? There is no one who is not familiar with the force developed in all revolving bodies. If a globe be attached to one extremity of a cord, while the other is retained in the hand, the moment the globe is set revolving it commences a struggle to break the cord, and free itself from the restraining hand. As the velocity of revolution increases, so does this developed tendency to fly from the center increase. If, then, a planet were located in space, at its appropriate distance from the sun, and receive an impulse capable of impressing on it the velocity due to its orbit, unrestrained by any central power, it would fly from its orbit and dart onward for ever through space in a direct line, never turning to the right hand or the left. What tremendous power, then, is necessary to bind these mighty worlds into their circling orbits! It is again useless to say that this is accomplished by the power of the sun. Matter is inert, it can have no power save what God shall give.

As well might we declare that it is the power of the bone and muscle of the brawny arm of the smith, that wields the ponderous sledge. Sever that same powerful arm from the body, the form is retained, the muscle and bone are there, but mind, the animating principle, is gone, and at the instant of its departure all power is dead. So sever the sun from the will of God, and in that vast aggregation of matter all power dies, its light fades, and the planets, loosed from God's controlling power, fly madly through the abyss of space.

Nothing short of Omnipotence can hold these flying worlds. These are, however, but the merest atoms of creation; all their combined masses flung into the sun would scarcely augment his bulk by an appreciable quantity; and yet this mighty mass, the sun itself, is no more quiescent than its attending satellites. It, too, is flying through space, impelled and guided by the same Omnipotent hand. Stretching yet farther into creation, we behold an amazing scene. Not a solitary star that fills the concave is at rest; all, all, from the blazing Sirius to the faintest particle of star-dust revealed by telescopic art, are careering onward through immensity. System rising above sytem; cluster above cluster; universe above universe; moving with majestic grandeur; all held by the right hand of God omnipotent. "He ruleth in the armies of heaven, and among the inhabitants of the earth."

It is, perhaps, less difficult to affirm the almighty power of the Architect of the Universe, than to demonstrate that in *wisdom supreme* has he reared this stupendous fabric. The mind is far more easily and obviously impressed with the evidences of power than of wisdom. Just as the resistless power of the steam-car forces itself upon our minds through the senses, while the evidence of the wisdom displayed in its complex structure, can only be derived from the steady application of the higher faculties of the mind; so a superficial examination of God's universe, demonstrates, through the senses, his eternal power, while nothing short of a comprehension of the celestial mechanism, can reveal the wisdom supreme displayed in its organization and arrangement.

Nothing short of a knowledge of the true system of the universe, can demonstrate the wisdom of God. There was a time when the human mind, vain of its penetration, conceived it had reached the true rendering of heaven's high record. Cycle and epi-cycle, equant and deferent, marked with terrible and cumbrous complexity, the movements of the celestial orbs, until even mortal genius rebelled, and boldly (if not blasphemously) asserted, that if this were an evidence of the wisdom of God, his mind could have better counseled this imagined omniscience.

Since, however, we have reached to a true knowledge of the celestial architecture, the mind, the deeper it penetrates, is the more powerfully impressed with the wisdom, vast, comprehensive, infinite, eternal, in which and through which the worlds were made.

Let us again call to mind the organization of our solar system. In the center is located the controlling orb. At varying distances from this common center, a multitude of worlds are revolving in reëntering curves until the most remote includes in its capacious orbit, an area whose diameter is 60,000 millions of miles. These globes are to be so arranged, that while each one is subjected to the influence of every other, yet their pathways shall never suffer a change beyond narrow and prescribed limits. Their orbits shall ever expand and contract, their velocities shall ever increase and diminish, the planes of their motion shall ever rock to and fro; but at no period in the ages which are to come, shall any change so accumulate as to affect the equilibrium of this complicated system. If about the sun it were required to launch a single planet, it might not be difficult to determine the direction and power of the primitive impulse, required to produce a determinate result. Indeed, release the planets and their satellites from the disturbing influences of each other, and it would not then be impossible to achieve the resolution of the problem of a perfect and everlasting equilibrium.

But this is not the condition of the problem in nature. There is but one God, so there is but one kind of matter. If the will of God energize the material of the sun, so does it equally energize the material of every planet. While to finite minds complexity reigns, to the infinite intelligence, the oneness of matter, the unity of law, form the essence and perfection of simplicity.

Let us proceed, then, in the examination of this sublime problem. Let a power be delegated to a finite spirit, equal to the projection of the most ponderous planet in its orbit, and from God's exhaustless magazine, let this spirit select his grand central orb. Let him with puissant arm locate it in space, and obedient to his mandate, there let it remain for ever fixed. He proceeds to select his planetary globes which he is now required to marshal, in their appropriate order of distance from the sun. Heed well this distribution, for should a single globe be misplaced, the divine harmony is destroyed for ever. Let us admit that finite intelligence may at length determine the order of combination; the mighty host is arrayed in order. Nearest the center is located the brilliant Mercury, and then the orb of Venus. Next stands this terrene globe, and beyond, the fiery Mars, and then a wondrous group of minute worlds, far within the circling orb of Jupiter is placed. Beyond Jupiter stands Saturn with his rings; still more remote is seen Uranus, and farthest of all Neptune stands sentinel on the outposts of this grand array. In one vast line of continuity, these worlds like fiery coursers, stand waiting the command to fly. But, mighty spirit, heed well the next grand step; ponder well the direction in which thou wilt launch each waiting world; weigh well the mighty impulse soon to be given, for out of the myriads of directions, and the myriads of varying impulsive forces, there comes but a single combination that will secure the perpetuity of your complex scheme. In vain does the bewildered finite spirit attempt to fathom this mighty depth. In vain does it seek to resolve the stupendous problem. It turns away, and while endued with omnipotent power, exclaims, " Give to me infinite wisdom, or relieve me from the impossible task!"

Here we have presented the simplest possible problem. Add to the earth its moon, to Jupiter his four satelites; to Saturn its wondrous rings, and eight revolving worlds; complicate the problem with ten thousand fiery comets; God has computed the perturbations of this complex system, through all its infinite configurations; through infinite ages which are past, and through endless ages which are to come. It is useless to rise to schemes of yet greater difficulty, for we must be satisfied, that nothing short of omniscience could have constructed a system so involved, so complex, and yet so perfect, in all its multitudinous parts.

And yet how utterly insignificant does this appear, when compared with the marshaling of the mighty host of heaven. Look up to that wondrous zone, begirt with blazing stars, scattered by millions throughout its populous domain. Here is a combination so vast, so profound, so multitudinous, that imagination fails to grasp its mighty boundaries, and yet all is in motion. Each one of these myriads has its appointed track; the wisdom of God hath looked through the wondrous maze from the beginning, and lo! even to the final period of all things, perfection reigns.

We rise to a third attribute of Jehovah, declared in the sacred writings. God is *unchange-*

able, " the same yesterday, to day, and for ever." If this be the teaching of revelation, it is no less the teaching of science. But for this, man could never have risen beyond the sphere of mute wonder. It is the fact that God is unchangeable, the same yesterday, to day, and for ever, that gives to the human mind the power to rise upward, through the works of nature, to the source of all power and truth. It would not have been more difficult for the infinite Creator, to have governed the universe, to have upheld its worlds, to have sustained the mechanism of matter, and the existence of life, without regard to any order, or without the dominion of any specific laws.

We do not sufficiently consider this important truth. I have elsewhere attempted to demonstrate, that the present construction of the universe, is specifically adapted to the education and elevation of the human intellect. To accomplish this the phenomena of nature must be governed by fixed laws, otherwise the possibility of predicting them could never exist. The will of the Almighty is then manifested according to modes which change not. Look for example, at the admirable uniformity of the rotation of our earth on its axis; look at the beautiful precision which marks the revolution of the planetary orbs: while there is variation infinite, there is never for one moment a relaxation of any of the supreme laws, according to which God has chosen to manifest his being and presence. In every atom he reigns supreme. Let man attempt to imitate this attribute of the Deity; let him apply his power to give uniformity to the rotation of the simplest machine, how soon does he discover, that his own will, though never so carefully guarded, is ever varying, his efforts are ever relaxing or augmenting, and he soon yields in utter despair, at attaining uniform results even for a single hour. But the will of the Supreme, moves the universe, while no stretch of scientific research has ever yet detected the slightest variation or shadow of turning,—ever perfect, ever divine.

In tracing the relative positions of the sun, moon, and earth, we have been able to penetrate the past, backward three thousand years. Their relative movements have been scanned, the earth's rotation on its axis, the moon's revolution in its orbit, the earth's annual circuit about the sun. These are so linked together, that any change ever so minute, is within the grasp of the powers of science.

In one instance, indeed, it seemed that the law by which the power of God is ordinarily displayed, must be modified in those remote ages of the world. The moon seemed to be slowly breaking away from its orbit. There was an evident augmentation of her mean velocity, from century to century, and her present position appeared to be at least three times her own diameter in advance of her computed place. The cause of this startling phenomenon was long and earnestly sought. Was it indeed true, that one of the elements of equilibrium was slowly wasting away? Should this be demonstrated, what terrible consequences did it involve? Nothing short of the final decay and death of the entire system; slowly, indeed, but surely, one by one, the planets must sink into the blazing sun, and the space which once flashed with their living light must become once again, the domain of darkness and of death.

But faith sustained the research. As God can not change, so the laws of his manifestation are, in like manner, immutable: this apparent deviation was finally traced to its origin, and revealed one of the most astonishing phenomena in the universe of God.

The moon's acceleration was found to be due to a gradual change in the figure of the earth's orbit, accomplished in a vast period of thousands and thousands of years, by the combined influence of all the planets. It is now, and has been, expanding for thousands of years, and will so continue to expand, until its figure shall become circular, when the same power will reverse its action, and the circular is again slowly reduced to the elliptical orbit. So long as the circuit of the earth's orbit is on the increase, so long will the moon's mean motion be accelerated; but when this shall have reached its limit, and contraction begins, then will the moon's motion lose, by slow degrees, the velocity it had gained, and once more, at the close of some millions of years, return to its primitive condition.

This is not a solitary example of these wondrous exhibitions of the invariability of the manifestations of God's power. Not an element, in all the planetary orbits, is absolutely fixed,— all is changing, yet ever in accordance with God's great law. The source of power is eternal, the law of its manifestation everlasting, and the decree has gone forth throughout the universe : Thus far shall your mighty fluctuations go, but no farther; the limits of vibration are fixed and immutable as the pillars of heaven.

We now proceed to the consideration of the *ubiquity* of God. "He filleth immensity by his presence," is the declaration of the sacred volume. How grand the idea, how sublime the conception! Could unaided, uninspired mind have risen to so wonderful a thought?

If we have been successful in presenting conclusive evidence of the being of a God; if this supreme intelligence is indeed the living spirit of the universe; if at his bidding the sun pours forth its ceaseless floods of light and heat; if by his almighty arm the worlds are projected and guided in their orbits;—then indeed, so far as creation extends, to the very outermost confines of inhabitable space, God dwelleth by his Spirit, exercising a positive, direct, immediate control over the works of his hands. As the spirit of man pervades every particle of his corporeal frame, enduing it with life, and energy, and power, so must the Spirit of God pervade every atom of created matter. Should he for one moment withdraw his sustaining power, not only would chaos come, but even matter itself would cease to be.

But let us examine, for one moment, how far we are warranted in the use of the sublime expression,—His presence filleth immensity. Once our knowledge of the universe was limited to a region of space so minute, that when compared with what has since been revealed, it seems but an inferior corner in the empire of God. Had this been all, had the stars visible to the naked eye constituted the entire universe, it would have been possible to have pierced far beyond these limits, and to have demonstrated that creation was finite. It is true that even the boundaries of such a kingdom are immense. It is computed, from data not to be questioned, that the eye has the power of discerning single stars at so great a distance, that their light can not pass it in less than a hundred years, though flying in every minute of time, twelve millions of miles; and yet, compared with the now visible boundaries of creation, this incredible and incomprehensible distance shrinks to an almost insensible point.

I will not here undertake to explain how it is that the telescope enables the eye to penetrate space. That this power belongs to this magic instrument, no one can doubt who has ever seen a small, feeble star, converted by optical power into a magnificent orb, forty times more extensive than the moon's surface, as viewed by unaided vision. Who could have divined the nature of the revelations which would be made by an instrument giving to the eye a depth of penetration a thousand-fold greater than it possessed by nature? If, indeed, the Creator is infinite, if his august presence filleth immensity, then we had a right to anticipate that, no matter how deep the eye of man might pierce the domain of space, a point never could be reached wherein the evidences of God's presence would not appear. Such has been the result of the application of the telescope to sounding the mighty depths of the universe. Every augmentation of power has served to reveal new wonders; every increased depth to which the eye has penetrated, has evoked from the viewless depths of space, millions on millions of shining orbs, until the imagination is overwhelmed as well by the teeming numbers as by the mighty distances to which these island universes are removed. Conceive, if it be possible, of an object so remote that its light, flashing with a speed which no mind can comprehend, should still occupy a million of years in passing the mighty interval by which it is removed! and yet there is evidence that we now behold with the most powerful tubes, objects even ten, twenty, or thirty times more remote. We yield the point, and, in humble adoration, repeat the language of the sacred book, He inhabiteth eternity, his presence filleth immensity, and of his kingdom there is no end!

Such, indeed, is the effect produced by the telescopic explorations of the universe, that man has ceased to doubt the infinitude of God's empire, and now limits his ambition to a deeper penetration into its grandeur, without ever indulging the thought that he shall by any power pierce beyond its mighty limits. Lo! these are a part of his ways, but the thunder of his power who can understand? No one can rise to a full comprehension of the majesty of the kingdom of God, who has not had some opportunity of employing in his researches high optical power. Language is inadequate to convey any just idea of the splendors which burst on the sight, as the silent stars by millions go trooping across the field of vision. Space is not by any means equally populous in all directions. There are regions occasionally presenting themselves in which not a ray of light illumines the gloom of what would seem eternal night, while on the very confines of these starless patches, bright and dazzling regions burst upon the vision.

After penetrating beyond the zone of the Milky Way (a universe of itself), other objects are descried, which, to any but the highest optical power, are but faint clouds of light, but under the focus of the great telescopes, reveal their composition, exhibiting aggregations of innumerable stars, so remote that only their combined light can penetrate the enormous distance. These can not be otherwise interpreted. Their magnitude must be beyond measurement, while the number of their objects is beyond computation.

These islands of light are already counted by thousands,—each, doubtless, a universe vast and populous as that with which our own central orb is specifically allied. Every accession of optical power transforms their hazy masses into figures of the most astonishing complexity. Some are seen under the form of enormous spiral shells, with convolution on convolution, with dense central masses glowing with splendor, each convolution streaked with brilliant patches, gradually developing a train of astonishing grandeur. Several of these scroll-shaped universes, have been revealed, and it has been surmised, with much appearance of truth, that even our own Milky Way, if it could be seen in a direction perpendicular to its broadest extent, would exhibit a figure of like character. What these stupendous spiral forms may indicate, is yet beyond the grasp of human intelligence.

Other clusters are found which present the globular figure, with evident condensation at the center; others, again, assume the figure of rings of hazy light, while in others there is no appearance of definite organization. This, in many instances, is no doubt due to the fact, that no optical power, however great, has thus far been sufficient to reveal the true forms of objects sunk in space, to such immeasurable depths. If we are amazed with the magnificence of these objects, if by them we are taught the vastness of God's empire, we are no less overwhelmed when we consider the number of individual objects which claim the special guardianship of Jehovah.

It is reckoned that not less than one hundred millions of stars are now visible, within the limits of the Milky Way. In case we admit that each of these stars is a sun, and that each is the center of surrounding planets, we are forced to admit the existence of a thousand millions of worlds, within the limits of one single aggregation, one great and populous cluster. Shall we say that but one of these thousand millions of worlds is filled with life and intelligence, and that one among the most insignificant? This would surely be utter madness. People, then, these millions of worlds with inhabitants, proportioned to their extent of surface, and how amazing is the number of the population of the empire of God!

We have, however, here only considered a single province. Multiply again by a thousand all we have said or seen, and we shall even then fail to reach the limit of actual telescopic revelation. Well may we exclaim, "The heavens declare the glory of God," while "the firmament showeth forth his handy-work."

Thus do we find abundant evidence, that the presence of the Most High filleth immensity. It is likewise declared, by the sacred writers, in many places, that Jehovah inhabiteth eternity;

his kingdom is from everlasting to everlasting, and of his dominion there is no end. No attribute of the Supreme is more inscrutable than his eternity. Without beginning, without end, self-existent, everlasting. God manifesteth himself in time, but he inhabiteth eternity. We can not undertake to demonstrate the eternal being of God from his works, which are not eternal. They had a beginning and may therefore have an end, but we are permitted to reason analogically, and while it is impossible to compass the idea of eternity, either past or future, we may at least expand our conceptions, by an examination of the mighty periods of time embraced within the range of the physical creation.

All is accordant in this mighty temple built "without hands, eternal in the heavens." If the universe, by the number and splendor of its orbs, by their masses and magnitudes, by the stupendous scale on which it is built, by the simplicity of the laws by which it is governed, declares in letters of living light, the being and attributes of the ever-living God, so do the periods of revolution worked out in the heavens demonstrate that with him a thousand years are as one day, and one day as a thousand years.

We are told that "in the beginning, God created the heavens and the earth," but who shall measure by mortal years, when that beginning was? We have evidence full and conclusive, in the rocky records of the earth itself, of the vast periods of time which have rolled away, since the dawn of creation began. If we interrogate the heavens, the same response is made. If it be true, that in case at this very moment, the entire universe of God were blotted from existence, all save the earth itself, that even now with our present telescopic power, the last object would not fade from our view for millions of years; then, indeed, we are forced to admit that millions of years have elapsed, since these remote objects were called into being, and their light darted on its infinite journey to the earth.

There is no escape from this conclusion. Let it not be thought that these teachings are in contradiction to the Word of God. In its appropriate place this subject will be fully treated, and if we are not mistaken, all seeming discrepancy will be removed. From these two sources, then, the earth and the heavens, we deduce a pre-existence of the universe, only to be reckoned by millions of years. If now we examine more clearly the periods assigned to the revolutions of the celestial orbs, we are amazed at the grandeur and sublimity displayed in the going-on of this divine machinery. Leaving the periods of the planets of our own system, we rise to an examination of the binary stars, and while some are performing their revolutions in periods of comparatively short duration, in others there is evidence, that a single revolution of one body around another is not completed in less than a million of years! This is but the revolution of an object about another. In case we proceed upward to more complex systems, these mighty periods of time expand and swell, till finally it seems that eternity alone can furnish the requisite ages, wherein a single revolution of the multiplied orbs of God's universe, may be completely effected, and all return to the points from which they were projected, to commence anew their mighty cycle of never-ending motion.

Thus, does time almost swell into eternity; and, if such be the creature, what must be the Creator?

We have thus, from an examination of the physical organization of the universe of matter, demonstrated the unity of God, his almighty power, his infinite wisdom. We have shown that he inhabiteth eternity, and that his presence filleth immensity. By his direct power the world was not only formed, but this same power is momentarily employed to sustain the vast superstructure, which has been reared in wisdom. Whence, then, we demand, did the writers of the Hebrew Scriptures derive their perfect ideas of the Creator of the universe? They never penetrated the arcana of nature. They never pierced with optic tube the realms of space. They never tracked the swift planet, or the fiery comet. They knew nothing of the mighty laws of matter, the modes of God's wonderful display. They had learned nothing of the vastness of the universe from positive inspection, and yet in the most wonderful manner, and in language which no tongue can equal, have they portrayed the attributes of God. Can any one answer this inquiry, without resorting to the hypothesis that this wonderful knowledge is the direct revelation of God? This, then, is our solution, this the only explanation which our feeble powers find it possible to present.

Examine the writings of the sages of antiquity, even the philosophy of the profound Roman and the subtle Greek. These had equal opportunity to reach to a knowledge of the attributes of their Jupiter Creator, but even the imagination heated by poetic fire, failed to picture forth more than the feeble shadowings of that grand, awful, and sublime Jehovah, portrayed in the sacred volume.

Shall we attempt to proceed further in our deductions from the structure of nature? There are certain attributes of the Deity, which perhaps the material universe can not reveal. The material kingdom of God is governed only by physical laws, and can not be affected by the attributes of divine love, divine goodness, divine mercy. It is only towards God's rational creatures that these affections of the divine mind can be exercised. We can not, however, affirm that the benevolence of the Supreme mind is not distinctly revealed in the physical constitution of our earth, and its allied bodies. When we examine the endless, admirable contrivances by which human happiness is extended; when we perceive the forms of grace and beauty which fill the earth; the wonderful pictures in clouds and in the landscape; the glowing tints of heaven, and the rich effulgence which sparkles on the earth, we are led to exclaim, that God is good! When we comprehend how intimately our being is interwoven with the fabric of material nature, the air we breathe, the sparkling fount that slakes our thirst, the rich and luscious fruits, and gentle breezes of earth, that give healthy vigor to our frames,—what must be the attributes of that Eternal intelligence which has called into being the matter of innumerable worlds, which has, with geometry profound, fashioned these countless systems; with compass and measuring line meted out their habitation, and appointed to each its abode in space?

Nature not only declares with voices innumerable, deep as the pealing of ten thousand thunders, the being of a God, but in all the pillars of her empire, in all the magnificence of her architecture, in her architraves and archways, in her star-lit domes of superlative grandeur, in the resistless motions of her multitudinous worlds, in the interminable extent of her empire, she proclaims the attributes of her omnipotent Creator and God.

These are the themes to which we shall next invite your attention.

LECTURE III.

THE COSMOGONY AS REVEALED BY THE PRESENT
STATE OF ASTRONOMY.

LECTURE III.

THE COSMOGONY AS REVEALED BY THE PRESENT STATE
OF ASTRONOMY.

THE most wonderful volume in existence is, beyond a doubt, the Bible. It is wonderful for its high pretensions, for its almost incredible claims to divine origin, for its exceeding antiquity. It is wonderful in its revelation of the being of God, and in its declarations concerning the attributes of this Almighty Spirit. It is wonderful for its professed revelation of the creation of the universe, the formation of man, the origin of evil, man's fall from innocence, and his restoration to happiness. It is wonderful for its daring chronology, its positive history, its prophetic declarations. It is wonderful on account of its sublime philosophy, its exquisite poetry, its magnificent figures, its overwhelming language of description. It is wonderful for the diversity of its writers, diverse in their attainments, countries, languages, and education. It is wonderful for its boldness, in the use of illustrations, metaphors, figures, drawn from every department of human knowledge, from natural history, from meteorology, from optics, from astronomy. It is wonderful for the superior conceptions of its writers, of the grandeur and magnificence of the physical universe. It is wonderful that it has exposed itself to attack and destruction, at every point of time, by every discovery of man, by the revelations of geology, chronology, history, ancient remains disemboweled from the earth, by astronomy, by the discoveries of natural history, and, above all, by the non-fulfillment of its historical predictions. And it is most of all wonderful, that up to the present time, in the opinion of hundreds of thousands of the judicious, reflecting, and reasoning, among earth's inhabitants, during three thousand years since its first book was written, it has maintained its high authority, and has retained in all this vast lapse of time a powerful sway over the human mind.

On all these accounts (exclusive of its moral teachings, its grand primary object), no one will deny that it is a volume demanding the most attentive and patient investigation. It has not escaped overthrow for lack of enemies. It has been assailed at every point,—its history, its theology, its chronology, its cosmogony, its astronomy, its geology, all these in their turn have been attacked by the cultivators of science, and by the onward movement and development of each succeeding age. The philosophy of Greece has departed. The hoary astronomy of three thousand years, has perished in the grave. The gods of antiquity, the Olympic Jupiter, the dazzling Apollo, the trident-bearing Neptune, and the forger of Heaven's thunderbolts, are all swept away by the onward heaving of the human mind, if not by the superior power of the revelations of this wonderful volume. And yet, the most venerable system of all remains, and to this system we are compelled by reason, by sound sense, by pure philosophy, to turn and inquire how this is, and whence the mystery of perpetuity and powerful tenacity of life. All else dies while the Bible survives. Even the nation from whence it sprang, the languages in which it was composed, the countries of its birth scarcely exist, but in its marvelous pages. If, indeed, it be the Word of the ever-living God, then, indeed, the mystery is revealed; but if this high claim can not be maintained, he who disbelieves must frame a theory by which the present facts may be reasonably explained.

It must be borne in mind that the books of this volume were composed at periods of time widely separated; a lapse of nearly 2000 years intervenes between the date of the compositions of Moses and the Revelation of St. John, the divine; and now nearly a like period has rolled away, since the sacred canon was closed, and the book was sealed up for ever, nothing more to be added, and from its finished contents nothing ever to be taken. It was closed up amid the spendors of the Roman empire, when literature, and art, and philosophy, held their golden reign over the civilized world. It was fully finished while yet science was in its infancy; during the reign of error, and ignorance, and prejudice, and long before the truths of science, in any of its departments, had yet shed their light upon the world. During these eighteen hundred years of the Christian era, for this volume has even given an era to the most cultivated nations of earth, the human mind has not been idle. In history it has searched the buried ruins of past centuries, it has disentombed mighty cities, colossal columns, endless hieroglyphs. It has read on coins, on medals, on inscriptions of the rocks, in monumental piles, in sculptured enigmas, the history of the past. The fragments of the primitive writers of all nations have been collected, the Egyptian Manetho, the Babylonian Berosus, the Phœnician Sanchoniathon,—all have been searched to fling their light far back into the dark clouds which engloom the past. Chronology has brought to her aid the discoveries of modern science, and the celestial revolutions have been marshaled in her service. Geology has upheaved the crust of the solid earth, and deep delving, she has dug up the remains of former generations. Plants and animals, insects and reptiles, the inhabitants of a primeval, preadamite earth, in their classes, orders, genera, and species, have all been brought under the bright focus of scientific investigation. Above the earth, science has soared into the clouds of heaven, and from her lofty height she has revealed the facts and phenomena which crowd earth, ocean, and atmosphere. The lightning's blaze and the thunder's peal, the soft dew, the gentle zephyr, and the blasting tornado, have all been studied. Far beyond in the blue ether she has winged her flight. She has pierced the bright canopy of heaven, and opened up the amazing universe which towers on every hand, lost, interminable in the unfathomable depths of space. In short, since the closing of the sacred canon, a new world has been revealed, and science on her uplifted throne, quadruple-crowned, sways a scepter over a boundless empire, which then had no existence. If, then, this so-called sacred volume be a tissue of falsehood, if its philosophy be false, its theology false, its morals false, its cosmogony false, its astronomy false, its history false, its productions false, its natural science false, its geology false, its chronology false, then indeed let it beware, for science is marshaling its forces with strength irresistible, pouring in from the east, west, north, and south; ascending from heights insurmountable, rising from depths unfathomable; all, all, conspiring the overthrow and final destruction of every system which is not founded on the solid rock of truth itself.

No one with a soul, which has ever risen above the clouds of prejudice, can for one moment regret the downfall of error. Who regrets the destruction of the philosophy of Aristotle, of the astronomy of Ptolemy? But it may be demanded is the Bible open to attack? Does it pretend to teach any system of science? Yes, it pretends to teach theology, morals, and religion, directly and positively, while it adverts indirectly to every branch of science, and in these occasional allusions, lays itself open to attack at a thousand points. It is again demanded, whether its writers did not studiously avoid any commitment, with reference to matters of pure science? In case this be true, then is it one of the most inexplicable of marvels, that each one of this multitude of writers, scattered along the shores of the descending current of time for two thousand years, each one as his occasion required, boldly reaching out his hand into the dark, and dragging to his use whatever of science his subject demanded, and yet with such wise caution, that the full blaze of truth and knowledge may never detect the ignorance of him, who thus plunges at random into the gloom of scientific night. It may be asserted that positive statements have been avoided in the simplest of ways,—that there were none known, to be made. But this is not the fact. Positive statements are made, and that too in the most unequivocal language. I need only cite the order of creation, the facts of history, the predictions of the future, the universal deluge; while to each of the other departments of knowledge there is constant reference.

The Bible, then, is open to attack—indeed, it is in no possible point guarded from attack. There is no shield but truth for its sacred character; there is no bulwark but truth to defend it from the assaults of its enemies; and if there be those who, after mature study of its pages, have reached the conclusion that this is the great volume of God's truth, surely it is just that the grounds of their belief should be set forth, that others may read, reflect, and decide. I proceed, then, without further delay, to consider the cosmogony of the universe as developed in the Mosaic history of the creation. Before it be possible to approach the discussion of this subject, we must make as clear a development as possible of the present state of our scientific knowledge, with reference to this deeply profound and mysterious subject.

The topics to which we now invite your attention, are among the most sublime that ever engaged the powers of an intelligent mind. Whence sprang this mighty universe of blazing suns? Whence these multitudinous worlds which circle round their central orbs, far flying through the deep of space, freighted with their numberless inhabitants? Were they brought into being by the fiat of Omnipotence? Did the command go forth, Let the universe be! and at the bidding of God, did sun and system, satellite and planet, and all the blazing host of heaven, and the mighty schemes which fill the deep profound, burst into sudden being, and flash their splendors throughout the startled empire of vacuity? Or is there a plan, wise, deep, and eternal, mighty as God, extensive as space, comprehensive as immensity, working backward through innumerable millions of ages deep into primeval time, and working forward, through countless revolutions of heaven's host, to ages in the future to which no mortal power of thought can penetrate? Which is the more consistent with what we are able to learn of the workmanship of God in this goodly world which we inhabit? Are there here manifested any sudden bursts of being, or is all progressive? Whence came the forests which clothe the earth? Whence the monarch oak which rears heavenward its thunder-scarred form? Does it spring into being, as leaps the electric spark from the dark bosom of the cloud? We know its origin; and though generations roll away as this gigantic tree slowly rears its crest, we are well assured of its beginning, and can affirm positively of its gradual development.

This is the universal analogy of all that claim existence upon the earth. Indeed, we may go still farther, and affirm that the crust of the earth itself is but the record of successive revolutions, marking the great epochs in the past history of the world. So far, then, as we are able to trace the direct manifestations of God in the mineral, vegetable and animal kingdoms, He works by means, and according to a plan. If we ascend to the organization of the solar system we shall perceive even here that it is built on a plan, and in accordance with certain great and governing laws. The same appears to be true of the various aggregations of stars, and of the mighty astral systems of space. This, however, is an examination made in the condition of maturity. It is like the exhibition of design in the structure of the full grown oak, already alluded to. We can not so surely trace the development of a system of worlds. We can not so certainly behold them forming under our eye; although possibly this process may at this moment be advancing. In case we could trace absolutely the formation of our single system from its primitive amorphous state, to a condition of full development, then we might with certainty extend these processes to all the systems already in existence; as this is impossible, at least in the present state of science, we are left somewhat to conjecture and speculation, though of course all speculation must be in accordance with the phenomena of Nature. We may frame theories and test them by facts, until their truth or falsehood shall have been demonstrated. I shall not stop to present the various theories which have been successively framed, to account for the existent condition of the planetary system. I shall confine my remarks solely to that one, which has of late years become somewhat noted, in consequence of its abandonment by certain prominent individuals, who had previously been its ardent advocates. It is the more notorious from the fact, that it has been employed as the foundation on which an extraordinary system of materialism has been constructed, involving the idea that creation is but a series of accidental and progressive developments. I allude, of course, to the celebrated nebular hypothesis of Sir William Herschel, better known as Laplace's theory, in consequence of the extension and application it had received from this learned French geometrician.

There are those, doubtless, who have conceived an aversion to this theory, in consequence of its supposed atheistic tendency. It would be highly unphilosophical to reject any theory on such a ground. If it be a mere speculation, unsusceptible of being brought to the test of actual discussion, then indeed its tendency to evil would be a valid reason for its rejection. After the repeated mistakes and blunders of the unlearned multitude, in these same matters, let us beware how we, in this age of progression, and freedom of opinion, plunge into like errors.

It was once thought that the doctrines of Galileo were at variance with truth and revelation. I presume there is no one at the present day who will undertake to assert that this same Copernican system is not firmly fixed on the foundation of truth, while revelation remains as undisturbed as though Copernicus had never lived.

Let us, then, abandon our prejudices, and, with philosophic and honest candor, examine the foundation on which this theory rests its claims to credence.

It is well known to all, that Sir William Herschel was the first who succeeded in the construction of powerful reflecting telescopes. He constructed one of these instruments of so enormous a magnitude, that in case its dimensions had not been surpassed in our own day, it would seem almost incredible that such an instrument could have been upreared, and directed to the examination of the celestial sphere.

The diameter of its speculum was no less than four feet, while the ponderous iron tube, was forty feet in length. With this gigantic instrument, possessing a power transcendently greater than that of human vision, concentrating as it did, the light from the most remote objects, on the pupil of its enormous eye, Sir William undertook a thorough review of the entire celestial region, visible in the latitude in which he was located. Objects of wonderful form and of most mysterious character not unfrequently presented themselves to his view, as they floated cloud-like across the field of his mighty telescope. They were not stars, they did not present the appearance of clusters of stars, they shone with a dim mysterious light, without definite outline, shadowy in their character, and only rendered more enigmatical, the more advantageous the circumstances under which they were viewed. These objects of which he discovered many hundreds, nay even thousands, he named nebulæ, and these he subdivided and classified, according to their distinctive characteristics. Among these we find resolvable nebulæ, those which are manifestly composed of stars, yet so distant that no optical power then in use, could disentangle the rays which were mingled in their vast journey to the earth. Others were termed planetary nebulæ, from their resemblance to a planetary disc. A very large class, in which no evidence of possible resolvability was found, were denominated amorphous nebulæ. Among these last, a great variety of objects existed: some were discovered so faint and delicate as scarcely to stain the deep blue of ether, and indeed were invisible to any but the most experienced eye, and even this eye must first have been subjected to powerful action of long continued and deep darkness, to develope its acutest sensibilities; others again were enormous in their magnitude, filling field after field of the instrument, with their shadowy forms pierced here and there by enormous cavities, jet black, and lighted up in spots with concentrations of greater splendor.

Many were the speculations which passed through the mind of the great discoverer as to the true character of these anomalous objects. He was familiar with the forms and appearance of the clusters of stars. Hundreds of these objects, which had resisted the power of all preceding telescopes, had been resolved into stars by his own great instruments. In the outset he naturally adopted the hypothesis, that all these hazy clouds of light, so profusely scattered through the regions of space, were nothing more than vast aggregations of stars, so deeply sunk in space as to defy the space-penetrating power of his largest-sighted telescopes. But a more extended examination finally led him to doubt, and at last a discovery broke in upon him, which drove him from this hypothesis, and led him to the formation of another, which is, perhaps, the boldest which human thought has ever conceived. The phenomenon which so riveted his gaze was the halo of this hazy, nebulous light, in whose center shone a well-formed and perfect star! How could this phenomenon receive an explanation on his old hypothesis? In case the shadowing envelope of this central star was itself but the aggregation of millions of stars, how vastly superior in magnitude and brilliancy over all the others must that central orb be, which so far outshone the millions of millions by which it was surrounded. On the other hand, in case we attribute to the central body a magnitude conformable with that of the other stars of heaven of equal luminosity, how utterly insignificant must be those countless stars, whose combined light appeared but as a faint, luminous atmosphere around the central orb?

This object, then, combined with a multitude like it, sustained by the various other phenomena of nebulous bodies, finally induced Herschel to adopt the notion, that matter manifested itself in the heavens in two distinct forms: first, as perfectly formed and solid stars, or suns and planets; second, in nebulous masses of chaotic and vaporous matter, enormous in extent, of exceeding tenuity, and in every way analogous to the trains of luminous particles which not unfrequently attend the more solid portions of the great comets which occasionally visit our system from the remoter regions of space.

As these vast masses of nebulous mist are known to concentrate and settle down upon the nucleus of the comet, it was not difficult to extend this idea to the possible condensation of the vaporous envelopes of the fixed stars upon these luminaries, and finally to rise to the thought that possibly this chaotic, nebulous, amorphous fire-mist might be the primordial condition of matter, and that the nebulous stars were specimens of the imperfectly condensed matter. This bold thought appeared to be abundantly sustained by succeeding investigations. The most marvelous forms were revealed, such as double nebulæ with condensing centers; double stars, with trains of interjacent nebulous matter, apparently under the positive, condensing power of each of the bright centers; nebulous masses, with partial condensation, about well-defined nuclei, having dark vacuities, through which shone the deep and distant heavens as through a window. Such, indeed, was the accumulation of evidence in favor of this astonishing theory, that Herschel at length promulgated his views to the world, and presented the evidences on which his opinions were based. He conceived that the all-prevalent power of universal gravitation was now actually exerting itself over these nebulous masses of matter, and that even now worlds were forming in the womb of space; while the myriads of bright orbs which fill the heavens had their origin in the same chaotic matter, wrought into form and beauty by the action of these same laws of universal gravitation. Here, then, was a cosmogony of the stellar heavens, far different from any thing previously propounded. It exhibited a mighty scheme of development. God's creative power had called matter into being. In its primitive, nebulous condition, it had filled the boundless expanse of space. The omnipotent Spirit had breathed upon this unfinished ocean, life had burst upon it, and the will of God, operative and manifested in the great law of gravitation, had commenced and carried forward, through the countless millions of ages of the past, the grand work of perpetual development.

The idea was at least sublime. There was nothing in it, as thus presented, to shock the feelings of the most devoted friend of the sacred volume. It was but another round mounted by the human mind, in its effort to ascend through Nature closer to the throne of Nature's God. It was in accordance with all the developments of the workmanship of God's fingers on earth. All else was progressive development, from the tender flower to the sturdy oak, from the most delicate insect to the gigantic Behemoth. Man, made in the image of God, received his strength and power, and wisdom, by slow degrees, and why should not the all-pervading principle extend itself, even to the glorious orbs that God has fixed in the heavens, to manifest his glory, and to make known the unsearchable riches of his wisdom and his power?

This most wondrous speculation seemed to be further confirmed by a multitude of facts. Among the nebulous stars, some were found, in which there was but a feeble concentration of light in the center of a luminous circle. In others the light was more developed; and thus onward a series would be formed, by individuals properly selected, until finally a brilliant star shone in the center of its gauzy envelope. As our own sun is one of the fixed stars, it was natural to inquire what was its condition,— whether it exhibited any trace of this strange phenomenon which the telescope had revealed in the heavens. About the sun it had been long known that an extensive atmosphere existed; but this was only analogous to the gaseous envelope of our earth and the other planets. A closer scrutiny of the sun detected a remarkable relation between this body and a faintly luminous appearance, long distinguished under the name of the Zodiacal light. This luminous beam, ever based upon the sun, and attendant upon its annual apparent movement, is visible with peculiar distinctness at certain seasons of the year, extending in an elongated, elliptic form to a vast distance from the sun, reaching even beyond the limits of the orbit of the planet Venus, and possibly to that of the Earth. Here, then, it seemed, was found, in actual existence, the remains of that primeval, nebulous globe from whence our sun had sprung, in the form of a vast gaseous atmosphere of exceeding tenuity, revolving with the sun on its axis, and extended to its lenticular form by the centrifugal force due to rotation. Such, then, was the condition of this great problem, as left by Sir William Herschel; and it was at this point that Laplace received it, and, by the force of his wonderful genius, extended the range of the speculation far beyond the limits imagined by its illustrious author.

Any theory which would account for the fixed stars and for the formation of the sun, would be greatly strengthened if, at the same time, it could be made to explain the planets, satellites, and comets, and embrace within its scope the peculiar phenomenon presented in the organization of the solar system. Whence came the worlds which circle round the sun? and whence the moons which subordinate themselves to the action of their central bodies? and, above all, whence spring those anomalous bodies which occasionally visit our system, and, after a brief sojourn, again disappear in the invisible regions of the universe? These questions had long been propounded in vain, and conjecture had been exhausted in its efforts to account for their origin.

It was to explain these phenomena that Laplace had recourse to the nebular theory of Sir William Herschel; and it is to the specific consideration of this subject I would now invite your attention.

In the outset of this discussion we must clearly distinguish between those phenomena, for which the law of universal gravitation is responsible, and those other phenomena of the constitution of the solar system, in the explanation of which this law has never been employed. Gravitation explains why the planets, comets, and satellites revolve in elliptical orbits, or in those curves known as conic sections, consisting of the circle, ellipse, parabola, and hyperbola. Gravitation explains the unequal velocities of these bodies in their orbitual movements. It, in like manner, explains the multitudinous perturbations suffered by all the members of the solar system, in consequence of their reciprocal action. In short, the system once organized as it now is, all its existent and daily occurring phenomena are susceptible of explanation and computation from the theory of universal gravitation. Here, however, the domain of this law is bounded,— or, at least, has hitherto been bounded. There remain a multitude of inquiries demanding answers, for which, however, gravitation has not been deemed accountable. For example, why do all the planets and satellites revolve in orbits so nearly circular? So far as gravitation is concerned, they might as well have revolved in parabolas or hyperbolas. Why do all the planets circulate about the sun in the same direction? Gravitation would have held them, all the same, in case they had moved in the opposite direction. How comes it that the planes of the planetary orbits are nearly coincident? Gravitation renders no reply to this question, and is not responsible for the answer. Again, the planets all rotate on axes in the same direction in which they revolve in their orbits. The satellites follow these same analogies, and even the sun himself is, in like manner, found to rotate on his axis, in the general direction of the motion of his attendant satellites. While this astonishing harmony and uniformity prevail with reference to the planets and their satellites, a far different order of things exists among the comets. These bodies visit our system from every possible region of space, under all angles of inclination, and revolve in any one of the curves already mentioned, except the circle. They do not pass round the sun in the same direction as the other revolving bodies, technically known as *the direct motion ;* but they exhibit as frequently the retrograde direction. Now, if this great scheme were formed by chance, and the planets and satellites had been projected in their orbits with forces of impulse and directions of motion solely determined by accident, there is not one chance in one hundred millions that the present organization would have been the result of such an origin.

The question then arises, may all these complicated phenomena presented in the solar system, be reduced under the dominion of a single law? and if so, what is the hypothesis which yields a satisfactory explanation of these multitudinous and diversified phenomena?

Laplace has furnished us the approximate answer to this grand inquiry. I present a rapid exposition of the great outlines of this vast speculation. It is believed that at one time the sun was a vast nebulous globe, of a diameter so great as to comprehend within its limits the orbits of all the planets. At this period there were no planets in existence, and the matter of which these bodies and their satellites are composed was, at this period, a portion of the mass of matter constituting that body which we now call the sun. In the lapse of ages, the mighty diameter of this primitive, globular body, exceeding six thousand millions of miles, is supposed to have slowly contracted, by the radiation of heat, into the regions of space. In case we admit the beginning of a rotation of the globular mass on an axis, the contraction of its dimensions must, by necessity, increase the velocity of rotation. If, then, the loss of caloric be ever continued, the contraction of the mass must be perpetuated, and the velocity of rotation will be ever increased, until a time will come when the centrifugal force, generated at the equator of the revolving mass, will preponderate over the force of gravity, and the particles of matter, thus acted upon in an equatorial zone, will be lifted up in a vast ring, and finally severed from the central mass. This cloudy, nebulous ring is then left in space, revolving on an axis coincident with that of the parent mass, and with a velocity exactly equal to that due to the central body at the moment it was disengaged.

The ring of matter, thus detached and left to the action of gravitation on its various particles, would not retain its primitive form; but its particles, concentrating about some center of superior density, would eventually assume the spherical form, and a planet would thus be formed.

This globular body, in its primitive condition a vaporous mass, by a more rapid radiation of its heat would ultimately solidify, and present all the phenomena of the solid globe we inhabit. In case we examine the peculiarities of condition of the imaginary planet thus formed, we shall find an astonishing similitude between it and those in actual existence. It must revolve in its orbit in the same direction in which the parent mass rotates. It must revolve in a plane nearly coincident with the equator of the central body. It must revolve in an orbit nearly circular. It must rotate on its axis in the same direction in which it revolves in its orbit. In each of these particulars, then, it fulfills the existing conditions of nature.

If now we follow the changes of the central rotating body, we shall find that the same causes which caused the evolution of the first ring of matter, must, in process of time, produce the same results again, and again, until a degree of condensation is reached bringing the powers of cohesive attraction to bear on the particles, and here all further disengagement of matter is for ever arrested. Condensation may continue, and an increase of rotatory velocity, but no more matter can be disengaged, because the attraction of gravitation is reënforced by the attraction of cohesion.

The generation of a scheme of worlds, under the operation of such laws and from such material, would produce a system, imitating in all its grand features those existent in the present solar system. Especially is this true, in case we extend the hypothesis to the formation of satellites around the primary planets, by the same process, which in the outset gave birth to the primary from the sun itself. All the moving bodies thus formed will revolve and rotate in the same direction, and in this they must harmonize with the rotation of the sun. They must revolve in planes nearly coincident with the sun's equator, and in orbits nearly circular, while the moons or satellites must follow the same general law.

Such, then, is the exhibition of this magnificent hypothesis. It can not be denied that it accounts for a multitude of phenomena hitherto inexplicable, and wonderfully expands our ideas of the majesty and grandeur of the wisdom of God. But it may justly be inquired, Is there any solid basis for this amazing superstructure? Is it mere speculation? or can any arguments or facts be adduced to give to it even the color of a reality?

We proceed to answer these inquiries. Are there now existent in the heavens any of these mighty nebulous globes, such as the sun is once supposed to have been? The telescope has revealed a class of bodies, called planetary nebulæ. They are in the region of the fixed stars, they have no sensible parallax, they have measurable diameters, are evenly shaded with light, and located at such stupendous distances, they swell to a magnitude almost incredible, in case we suppose them to be masses of vaporous or nebulous matter. Their diameters must even surpass the diameter of the orbit of Neptune, the most remote of all the solar planets, and the one first disengaged from the sun, in case no exterior planet exists. We do not affirm positively that these planetary nebulæ are globular masses of nebulous matter. They, however, exhibit many of the characteristics of such globes, and admit of this explanation more readily than of any other of which I am aware.

Again, in the heavens we find vast aggregations of luminous haze, resembling in every particular, chaotic, amorphous masses of nebulous matter. It can not, indeed, be positively asserted that any one of these masses shall never be converted, by telescopic reach, into stars, though it will be found, I think, at this time, that there are few distinguished astronomers who will deny that nebulous clouds do exist in the heavens. If, however, the actual existence of matter in this nebulous condition be essential to give a real basis to this theory, may we not find it abundantly exhibited in the trains of light which sometimes accompany comets, and which occasionally extend a hundred millions of miles. The rarity of these masses is of the most surprising character. I have, on some occasions, examined the most minute telescopic stars, and have received their light undimmed, though it had penetrated thousands and tens of thousands of miles of this cometary matter.

We have, then, actually existing and under our eye, the condition of matter required by the hypothesis,—and this is truly matter, and subject to the laws of motion and gravitation, as has been abundantly shown from the computed movements and revolutions of these nebulous masses. Furthermore, the directions of the motion of comets, the planes of their orbits, their physical condition, and the curves in which they revolve, appear in a remarkable manner to lend plausibility to this theory. In case we admit the formation of our sun from a nebulous mass, we must extend the same theory to the stars, which are also suns; and hence it will arise that in the concentration of matter into mighty globes, about certain centers of attraction, there will be fragments of matter occupying regions of space, in the interstices of these primordial globes, which will be long held in equilibrio by the united attraction of the masses by which they are surrounded. A time finally comes when a preponderance determines in favor of the attraction of one sun above all others, and towards this one the nebulous mass slowly begins to move. An acceleration of motion follows every decrease of distance, till, finally, a strange body of portentous appearance invades the heavens, and we behold a comet descending perpendicularly, or with any obliquity to the ecliptic, and plunging apparently with incredible velocity into the sun. In case its direction of motion be not exactly to the sun's center, it will sweep round this body, and receding from the center, finally revisit the region of space from which it emanated. Thus we perceive that, in case this be the true origin of comets, they ought to visit us from every quarter of the heavens, their motions should be direct and retrograde, and their orbits ought to be elongated ellipses, or possibly hyperbolas or parabolas.

It may still be demanded, in case these primeval rings are the origin of the planets and satellites, why may not some single specimen yet remain as proof positive of this incredible hypothesis? Here, again we are able to declare, by the aid of the telescope, that these rings appear to exist. If it were possible to direct your vision to the planet Saturn, through a tube of superior power, you would behold an exhibition of exquisite beauty. You would perceive a luminous globe of vast dimensions, belted with stripes, and exquisitely shaded from center to circumference; but, more wonderful, you would behold, engirdling this planet, a broad and lustrous ring of light, of oval figure, and exhibiting the most beautiful curvilinear outline. Here are two, possibly three, of the primitive rings, now existing in space, and separated from their primary central planet. These rings are of great dimensions. The exterior diameter of the outer ring is nearly two hundred thousand, while the inner edge of the nearest ring is separated some twenty thousand miles from the body of Saturn. These rings are revolving with swift velocity, about an axis coincident with that of the planet, and in every particular corresponding to the hypothesis, that they were at some period far back in the history of time, disengaged by centrifugal force from the body of the planet, and left revolving in space. It is about Saturn especially that we might expect to find rings, if anywhere in the solar system. It is of vast dimensions; its specific gravity is scarcely greater than that of cork; it has a multitude of satellites (no less than eight) revolving exterior to the rings, the nearest one approaching very closely to the surface of Saturn, and performing its revolution around that body in a few hours. The matter composing the rings must then have been greatly condensed (comparatively) when severed from the planet, and would, if ever, retain its primitive form. The conditions of the equilibrium of these rings are of great complexity, and speaking as finite beings, it would seem utterly impossible that the rings could have been built and adjusted to the planet after its projection in space. It is true that, at the bidding of God, these stupendous circles of light could have started into being, and at the same command have taken up their present astonishing relations to the world they encircle. But this is contrary to the analogy of God's creative providence. The more we study this astonishing organism, the more are we convinced that these appendages must have been evolved from the central orb by the action of some great law, effecting in their severance all the conditions of permanent equilibrium. I never behold this resplendent system without feelings of awe and admiration. When I reflect how delicately these stupendous arches are poised in the heavens, how slight a cause would destroy their stability, it seems possible that even under one's eye the balance may be lost, and the whole fabric rush into utter and hopeless ruin! Indeed, so difficult is it to render a satisfactory account of the stability of these rings when regarded as solid (as they have been considered), that a distinguished American geometer has reached the conclusion by mathematical reasoning, that these rings are not solid but fluid, and that their particles are free to move among each other, that in this way the figures of the rings are for ever changing, swaying to and fro, like the ocean tides, to the action of the disturbing forces, which, if the rings were solid, might drag them from their orbits, and hurl them on the body of the planet, never again to be separated from it. We are not yet quite prepared to adopt this startling view of the system, while the facts announced show, beyond a doubt, the exceeding perplexity which hangs over this beautiful but enigmatical system.

If now we return to the examination of the actual condition of the great center of our system, we do not find any fact which can weaken the testimony already adduced. On the contrary, we are struck with the concurrent testimony presented by this central orb. Its stupendous magnitude is the first thing which strikes us; its intense heat, so infinitely superior to that of any planet; the lowness of its specific gravity, only one quarter as great as water; the vast extent of the atmosphere by which it is surrounded,—all conspire in testimony to the possible truth of the nebular hypothesis. But, above all, we are struck with the wonderful fact of the slow and majestic rotation of the sun on his axis! How astonishing is this! Why should this mighty orb rotate? We can see why the planets should revolve on their axes;

we can understand why the earth we inhabit should successively present each of its faces to the sun. In this motion of rotation we perceive the ultimate cause of the vicissitudes of day and night, so necessary and so grateful to earth's inhabitants, and by analogy we may extend this same reasoning to the planets; but nothing of a like character can carry our reasoning to the sun. Its gravitating power would be just as great without rotation; its floods of light would be just as inexhaustible without rotation; its vivifying heat would fructify the earth, and give life to the animal and vegetable world just as well without rotation. Every function of this mighty center would be just as perfectly performed in case it were absolutely fixed and immovable. We again ask in wonder, Why does the sun in twenty-eight days perform a complete revolution on its axis? No answer can be given, unless we revert for explanation to the seemingly bold speculation we are discussing. Admit this strange theory, and all difficulty disappears; and in the rotation of the sun we find the ultimate cause of the admirable scheme of revolving worlds by which it is surrounded. The rotation on an axis, now, is but the necessary concomitant of this higher function of the sun. If this theory be false, in how many different ways might its falsehood have been made manifest. Suppose we had found the period of rotation of the sun on his axis to be longer than that of any one of the surrounding planets in his orbit: this would have falsified the theory. Suppose we had discovered that it required more time for Saturn or Jupiter to rotate on their axes, than for their nearest moon to revolve round them in its orbit: this would have falsified the theory. Suppose we had found any planet or satellite revolving slower than the one exterior to its orbit: this would have destroyed the theory. No one of these phenomena has been observed. On the contrary, there is an admirable harmony everywhere existent, and all concurring to give the appearance of probability to this seemingly wild hypothesis. The sun, then, in all its phenomena, accords with the theory. We have already mentioned the phenomenon attendant on the sun, and called the Zodiacal light. This, as has been said, was conjectured to be an immense atmosphere surrounding the sun of uncondensed nebulous matter. A deeper penetration into the phenomena of the showers of meteors denominated the shooting stars, seems to connect, in a definite manner, these exhibitions with the revolution of a vast *nebulous ring*, revolving in space, and at certain seasons approaching sufficiently near the earth's atmosphere, to detach fragments of its body, and to fire them by their swift velocity through this comparatively dense resisting medium. Should this theory be adopted, we have among the primary planets a specimen of a primitive ring, still retaining its nebulous character, and of such exceeding tenuity as scarcely to be visible except under the most favorable circumstances.

Can it be possible, then, that the firm and solid globe we inhabit could ever have resembled so ethereal a body? Was there ever a period in the past when the material of this earth constituted a vast nebulous ring? Could this ring ever have been converted into a globular mass a half a million of miles in diameter? May the moon that now floats in space, two hundred and forty thousand miles from the earth, ever have been a portion of its mass? These are the marvelous questions demanding an affirmative answer, in case we adopt the nebular hypothesis.

When we examine the rocky crust of the earth, and perceive its density and solidity, we are almost disposed to doubt the possibility of its ever having been different. But we must not be governed too much by appearances. There is not a rock nor a metal, however solid, that heat will not dissipate into vapor. Even the diamond itself may, by heat, be made to float in the atmosphere. Indeed, the solids are only peculiar combinations of gases. Analyze the materials of the three great kingdoms of nature, and we reduce them all to gases. The waters of the ocean are composed of two gases; the rocks, mostly composed of gases; the vegetables principally composed of gases;—in short, we know that one single gas, oxygen, constitutes nearly, if not quite one half, of the solid material of the earth now known to man.

The rapid transitions of bodies from the gaseous form to the liquid, and from the liquid form to the solid, is too familiar to all to require more than a passing notice. Heat, then, is the all-powerful solvent of all organic matter, and by heat the solid earth itself may be again dissolved; and if so, why may we not believe that, by the same agent, its now solid materials once were held in solution, constituting the vaporous mass demanded by the nebular hypothesis.

Here, then, we might rest the discussion of this subject, with the conclusion that enough has been said to demonstrate the possible, if not the probable truth of this (at first sight) impossible theory. But we must yet advance one step further, and present an argument which, when combined with all we have said, so cements the whole into one mass of concurrent evidence, that, until a better theory be advanced, it seems impossible longer to reject the nebular hypothesis.

Within a short time a remarkable relation has been discovered to exist between the periods of rotation of the planets on their axes, and their masses, or quantities of matter and distances from each other combined. This relation is too technical to be stated here in mathematical language. We present the following popular exposition of the principle : If the quantity of matter contained in each of the three planets, Jupiter, Saturn, and Uranus, was accurately known, and their mean distances from the sun perfectly determined, then the principle of the new discovery would enable us, from these data, to compute or predict the exact time in which Saturn (the middle planet of the three) would revolve on its axis.

The earth's period of rotation on its axis is then dependent on the quantity of matter in the planets Venus and Mars, and upon the distances of the orbits of these planets from the orbit of the earth. . This is perhaps one of the most astonishing facts ever revealed. That Mars and Venus should sway the earth in its orbitual motion, results necessarily from the law of universal gravitation. But how, or in what way, these far-distant planets could ever have exerted the slightest influence in determining the period of the earth's rotation, is a mystery of mysteries, and but for the solution rendered by the nebular hypothesis, would seemingly remain an enigma for ever.

At this moment we are absolutely certain that neither one nor the other of these planets exerts the smallest influence on the earth's period of rotation. It is uniform, and has been invariable for two thousand years, while these planets have taken up every possible position relative to the earth. If, then, the velocity of rotation of the earth ever was dependent on their action, as this discovery demonstrates, we must go very far back in the history of creation to learn how that primordial influence might have been exerted. The subject is difficult. Permit me to illustrate. Suppose we should find a piece of machinery, in which there were three horizontal wheels revolving on vertical axes, near each other but not in contact. We examine the motions of these three wheels, we measure their diameters, and we find that their periods of rotation are precisely such as they ought to have been, provided that they once were in contact, and that a motion given to one had by it been communicated to the others. This exact relation existing, we should be strongly tempted to believe that the primordial state of these wheels was the contact of their circumferences, and hence arose the beautiful relation between their diameters and periods of rotation.

This merely illustrates the idea of working backward from present relations to those which possibly existed at some distant period in the past history of the bodies related. Let us now come nearer to the case of nature.

There is no one who may not have noticed the beautiful ring of steam which is occasionally ejected from the escape-pipe. It rises in the form of an annulus or ring, and floats sometimes for several seconds in the atmosphere. The particles of this annulus and the matter of the entire ring itself, are all revolving in the plane of the ring. Now suppose two other such rings, the one interior, the other exterior to the one first imagined; the three are now revolving, mutually affecting each other by actual contact of their particles upon their circumferences. Suppose these rings to contract by loss of heat, till finally they are severed from each other, and at last each breaks, its form condenses into a small globe, and three little planets are formed. Now the effect of their original condition of actual contact, can never be lost. Its impress is left, and possibly the rotations of these imaginary planets will have been so modified by such primitive contact as to remain, the perpetual evidences of this original, primordial condition.

Such, then, seems to be the case with the planets of our system. In their primitive condition, as immense annuli of gaseous matter, their circumferences once were in physical contact. The quantity of matter in each, and their relative diameters, would determine the influence that each would exert on the particles of the other. This influence has determined the periods of rotation, and these periods are now so related to the masses and distances of the interior and exterior planets, as to perpetuate for ever the astonishing evidence of their primitive condition.

Doubtless much remains yet to be done to develop fully this and other matters of like import bearing on this subject. But this much must be allowed, that the farther we advance, the deeper we penetrate the arcana of Nature, the more emphatically does it declare the probability of the truth of the nebular cosmogony of the universe.

If it should now be found that this theory coincides, as far as we can understand, with the Mosaic account of creation, we can safely pronounce that in this particular, in the present state of astronomical science, the revelations of Nature and of that book which professes to come from God, are not at variance. It is to the consideration of this subject we next invite your attention.

LECTURE IV.

THE MOSAIC ACCOUNT OF CREATION COMPARED WITH
THE COSMOGONY OF THE UNIVERSE AS REVEALED
IN THE ACTUAL CONDITION OF ASTRONOMY.

LECTURE IV.

THE MOSAIC ACCOUNT OF CREATION, COMPARED WITH THE COSMOGONY OF THE UNIVERSE AS REVEALED IN THE ACTUAL CONDITION OF ASTRONOMY.

"In the beginning God created the heavens and the earth." This is the sublime declaration of an historian whose writings are nearly a thousand years anterior to those of all others now in existence. It is the opening declaration of that wonderful volume which professes to have come from the ever-living God. It was recorded more than three thousand five hundred years ago. It was written at a time when darkness, deep, impenetrable, covered the nations of the earth, and at a time when from one extremity of the peopled globe to the other, no true knowledge of the universe prevailed. Read the language. Mark well the words. Observe their order of arrangement. "In the beginning." Not six or sixty thousand years ago; not six natural days prior to the creation of Adam; not on the first day of the earliest age, some millions of years backward, as the Hindoos assert;—but simply,—in the beginning. Mind, on the swiftest and strongest pinions of thought, may strive in vain to comprehend the meaning of that term. Who shall set limits and bounds to the creative energy of God? Who shall say that, from all eternity up to within that point of time, six thousand years, no act of creation had been put forth by divine omnipotence? Moses did not thus dare to circumscribe the powers of the Almighty. He declares that in the beginning, when in the wisdom of God creation was to begin, the fiat went forth, and God created the heavens and the earth. Jehovah is the agent in this grand drama of Nature. Whether a spiritual universe then existed, we know not; whether thrones, dominions, princedoms, virtues, powers, the spiritual hierarchs of heaven, were then present to celebrate this new development of divine power, we know not: we are only told the work was God's exclusive, almighty effort. It was a creation,—a calling into being that which had not previously existed. It was not an organization of existent chaos. There was no chaos, so far as matter is concerned; boundless, interminable vacuity reigned throughout the empire of space. But a new era was to dawn. Material creation was now to commence. The beginning of time was attained. The on-going of eternity was interrupted, and an unknown display, grand, magnificent, unutterable, was now to be made to the angelic spirits, if such then existed.

"God created the heavens and the earth." Mark well the order. The more exalted and dignified takes rank. Not the earth and the heavens, but the heavens and the earth. And now what was this creation thus briefly but sublimely announced? Was it indeed an instantaneous peopling of space with the mighty globes that now move and shine? Did space, on the instant, flame and blaze with myriads of glorious suns and revolving planets? Were these wondrous orbs instantly projected into space, and taught to describe their amazing paths? Was the solid earth, moulded in the Creator's hand, launched upon its never ending career? All this is impossible. No such announcement is made; and the very reverse of all this is true. The first grand act was the calling into being the matter, out of which and from which the heavens and the earth were to be fashioned and formed. It was the first, glorious, stupendous act of physical creation. It was bringing into being that which had not previously existed, the provision of inexhaustible material from which a universe was to be formed.

This is abundantly demonstrated in the succeeding declaration, in which we are told that the earth was without *form*, and *void*. How could this earth have been without *form*, if it had been already fashioned as a globe? How could it be void, if its solid rocks already rubbed its sides, and its huge mountain ranges lifted their barriers to the clouds. The earth was without form, and void. The matter for its future formation existed, but as yet no fashioning had been accomplished,—all was without form. Primordial atoms filled the deep profound. God was the mighty center; Infinitude alone could tell the boundary. "And darkness rested on the face of the great deep." What deep? Not surely the ocean, for as yet there was none. It was the great deep of unfathomable space; a deep so profound that no line can fathom its profundities, no eye but God's can penetrate its dark domain.

Here, then, it would seem, is pictured forth, in language not to be misunderstood, a primitive form or condition of matter, a primordial existence, anterior to sun, or planet, or blazing star. Darkness rested on the face of the great deep, and yet in the beginning God created the heavens and the earth. How, again I ask, can this be construed to mean the visible heavens, and existent earth, if darkness yet rested over the great deep? Every expression is positive and absolute; and whether there is revealed in the physical heavens or not, any evidence of the fact that matter once filled the capacious womb of space, in some existent condition, unclothed with any of its present attributes, this is assuredly asserted, if we can read aright, by the sacred historian.

Let it be further remarked, that the word here translated "created," is nowhere else employed throughout this narrative. There was but one creation, and that was of matter, and in the beginning. From all which we draw the conclusion, that Moses asserts that the matter of which the existent physical universe is built, was once without form, and void, filling with its ultimate particles the boundless domain of space, while darkness covered the face of the great deep!

Such, then, is the first grand act in the drama of creation. Matter is now existent, but formless, motionless, void, filling immensity, waiting the next high command from Him who called it into being. "And the Spirit of God moved upon the face of the waters." Then it was that matter first felt the vivifying power of God. We can not for one moment conceive that the waters of the ocean are here alluded to. It was the vast ocean of matter which filled the boundaries of space. This fathomless, interminable ocean, without limit, without bounds, this it was on which the Spirit of God moved, and gave to each particle of matter its now eternal function. Then first each particle of this vast unformed universe of matter felt and acknowledged the attractive power of every other; universal gravitation asserted its empire, and God's Spirit taught the ponderable particle the laws of motion.

"And God said, Let there be light; and there was light." How simple, how sublime, this stupendous declaration! Well may the Greek have marked its power and recognized its grandeur. God uttered the command, and quicker than thought the light-giving principle, the law of production and propagation of this great mystery, fills the universe of space. Struck by the moving atoms, its billows heaved in gentle undulations, and borne on its crested billow, light yet struggling in gloom spread feebly through the abyss of space.

The mighty reservoirs of light, which now flame on high, did not exist. There was as yet no sun to flood with light the boundless regions of his domain; the stars were not; and yet without these, " God said, Let there be light, and there was light."

Now, if this book be an imposture, a cunningly-devised fable, how marvelously has it been devised. How utterly irreconcilable with all the apparent phenomena of nature, to proclaim the creation of light prior to the formation of sun or star. Why was this? How can it be accounted for, if we suppose the description to have originated with mere man. Moses was learned in all the wisdom of the Egyptians. He was a poet, a legislator, a philosopher. How, then, was he induced to put forth a system of creation so utterly at war with the outward, palpable appearances of nature.

This same subject has perplexed the wisest commentators. Some, like Milton, have had recourse to an extraordinary fiction.

> * * * And forthwith light
> Sprung from the deep, and from her native east,
> To journey through the airy gloom began,
> Sphered in a radiant cloud. * * *

By this wonderful device, of which Moses says nothing, light is made to journey from east to west, and thus produce the change of day and night. I can not but feel such an hypothesis to be not only unnecessary, but degrading. For what purpose should light now be throned in "a radiant cloud?" to take up a journey about a non-existent earth? to produce an evening and morning, when the evening and morning now marked by men could have had no being.

Are we not led to higher thoughts by this sublime announcement? We know not what light is. Thus far God has chosen to conceal the character of this grand effect. One thing, however, seems to be certain. There exists throughout all space a medium or elastic fluid, imponderable, intangible, whose undulations, excited by certain bodies, produce the phenomenon of light. At the command of God, "Let there be light," this ethereal fluid filled the universe, and between it and the particles of matter a law of rotation was instantly established, by which the faint dawn of the morning of time broke upon the universe. It was the beginning of a great day, one of the mighty days of eternity,—a day which has grown brighter through all past revolving ages,—a day that can only end when God shall bid the physical universe depart, and all shall be spirit again!

In this dim portraiture of Moses, we perceive a strange accordance with the order of creation, as derived from our preceding investigation. After the creation of matter, and the enactment of the great laws of motion and gravitation, the production of light should follow next, in the grand progressive movement. But let us not here mingle cause and effect. It was because God commanded, that light was. Light would not have followed as a consequence of the condensation of matter, for there would then have been no vehicle for its transmission; and therefore there could have been no light. For its production, two things are required,—the elastic medium, and bodies to set this medium in motion with the required velocity of undulation. All matter does not possess the power of causing the elastic medium to undulate with such velocity as to produce light to the human eye. For its use a very restricted limit of vibration is required. For some eyes this limit may be extended, for others it may be contracted. But the grand principle God called into being, when he said, "Let there be light."

The severance between light and darkness is far more absolute than is apparent from a casual examination. The laws of vibration of the elastic medium, by whose undulations light is either formed or propagated, must fall within very restricted limits; hence, by the enactment of these laws of action, God separated most emphatically between light and darkness. We are moreover informed that " God saw the light that it was good;" the laws established were perfect; this medium by which the existence of the physical universe was to be revealed to intelligent beings, had already commenced its flight through space. The result was in accordance with the will of the Divine Architect, the end was accomplished, perfection reigned.

And now we are told, " God called the light Day, and darkness he called Night." The introduction of this passage, in so grand and sublime a description, occasions some degree of perplexity. At the time this naming of day and night took place there was neither the one nor the other. There was no sun, and no earth; and if any naming actually took place, it could only have been in anticipation. If we might be permitted slighty to paraphrase the passage, its accordance with the statements with which it stands connected, would be complete, while an appropriateness is at once evident for such an additional explanation. Had the passage been written, And God called the light *what we call* Day, and the darkness *what we call* Night, then it becomes a simple explanation of the meaning of the terms, light and darkness, and all perplexity is removed.

This closes the account of the first grand epoch in creation. Matter was called into being, the laws of gravitation and motion were established, and functions of all the varying particles of matter had been assigned. The vast and incomprehensible machinery for the production and propagation of light was finished; light itself had sped at the bidding of God from the center to the circumference; all was perfect;— and here closes the first great period. The evening and the morning, the beginning and the ending, the night, of ancient vacuity was closed, and the morning of a new creation had dawned; the first day, the primary period of time was now complete.

Such, at least, is the interpretation which is possible. Great perplexity has arisen from the use of the word day in this connection. If we understand by the term day a period of twenty-four hours, such as now exist, the statement of Moses is perfectly inexplicable. The writer knew as well as we do, that a day,—a natural day,—is produced by the *apparent* revolution of the sun about the earth. This is a matter of vulgar observation; and he could never have so far lost sight of the possibility of his account of this wonderful event, the creation of a universe, as to speak of the natural evening and morning constituting a literal day, to terminate the work of God, when there was no possible means by which a day could be produced. The word translated Day, can not, then, as here employed, mean a period of twenty-four hours. Indeed, we are informed, in the Second Chapter of Genesis, that "these are the generation of the heavens and of the earth, when they were created, in the *day* that the Lord God made the earth and the heavens." Here it seems to be announced that the work was finished in one day, as the same word is used in the singular. We are compelled, then, to believe that the word translated day, is a mere expression of a period of time of indefinite duration, and may extend to millions of years. This usage accords well with the customs of all ancient nations in the varied application of terms designating periods of time. We find a like latitude among the Hindoos, the Babylonians, the Egyptians, adopted by the Greeks, and copied by the Romans. The Egyptian Zaros seems to have had several distinct applications to periods of time, of different values. So, also, the use of the word, "year," in Latin "annus," a ring, a circle, or revolution, has been extended among the ancient nations to all possible periods of time. It is not then at all surprising, that an indefinite period of time should have been designated by Moses under the word translated, *day*. There is an objection urged against this interpretation and use, growing out of the enactment of the Sabbath, which we will consider more at length before closing this examination. We now proceed to consider the Mosaic account of the second grand period in the creation.

"And God said, Let there be a firmament in the midst of the waters, and let it divide the waters from the waters. And God made the firmament, and divided the waters which *were* under the firmament from the waters which were above the firmament; and it was so." In this passage we find the effect of imperfect knowledge of nature upon the minds of the truly great and learned men to whom we are indebted for our received translation. The old idea of a firmamentum, a something solid, like the crystal, transparent spheres of the ancients, clung to the human mind long after the absurdity was exploded in the minds of a few philosophers. The word translated "firmament," means, as is well known, an extension, an expanse, a sort of severance or vacuity, rather than any thing solid or firm; and in this sense, of course, we must consider it. Again, the word translated "waters" can not in any way refer to seas, oceans, and rivers on the earth, and to clouds and mist which float in the atmosphere above the earth. There were no waters such as now exist, and no earth such as we now inhabit. How, then, are we to understand this announcement of the work accomplished by the Almighty Architect during this second period of creation ? Suppose it had been written, "And God said, Let concentration of matter now proceed,—let the boundless ocean of material vapor divide and separate,—let vacuity intervene between the mighty masses which shall aggregate and segregate about their appointed centers,—and let this expanse be divided between the masses which shall lie above the expanse and those which lie beneath it,"—this would have been in so many words a description of the mighty processes which must have distinguished the period which immediately followed that one during which matter was created and the laws of matter established. At the bidding of God, under the controlling power of those laws by which He is pleased to manifest His divine will, and around centers of His own selection, the germs of future worlds were now beginning to form. Previously matter had been diffused like a boundless atmosphere, a material mist filling all space. Now aggregation begins and proceeds, severing this infinite nebulous mass into definite portions, an expanse divides these aggregations, concentration proceeds, and we perceive that an entire day, a vast period comparable with that which elapsed during the enactment of the first great act, rolls away while the work of separation and segregation proceeds.

Here was truly a grand and magnificent work. The selection of the great centers of aggregation was the work of Omniscience. These must be so located that the forming worlds shall in no degree interfere with each other. They must be so selected that in the development of the mighty systems to be brought into being, there should be space commensurate with the grand movements which were to be evolved. Matter was not left to itself. God was in all and over all; His wisdom sketched the mighty plan of creation on a scale commensurate with the glory and majesty and grandeur of His divine perfections.

Let us now examine the condition of the universe at the close of the second great epoch. If the division was perfected, in multitudes of instances at least we may conceive that the condensation had proceeded not only sufficiently far to produce vast globular bodies, but that these globes had condensed, and in the act of contraction and condensation, the planetary bodies may have been disengaged from their equatorial regions. There were then huge central masses of nebulous matter, slowly rotating on their axes, about these revolved hazy rings of matter, or possibly the crude forms of imperfectly condensed planets. Light was more condensed, and the grand centers of illumination were gradually increasing in power.

We are thus prepared, by the now nearly perfected operations, having this division and concentration of matter for their object, for the ushering in of a new and wonderful era in creation. The evening and the morning closed the second day.

With the opening of the third epoch we are introduced to the definite organization of the planetary worlds, and especially of our own earth. Its globular form had already been moulded. "And God said, Let the waters under the heaven be gathered together into one place, and let the dry land appear; and it was so." The boundless ocean, without limit and without shore, which had hitherto enveloped the earth, and the dense and misty vaporous atmosphere, retreated within narrower bounds; upheavals reared the mighty continent; and the chains of lofty mountains and the ocean's bed were formed; and the decree went forth, "Hitherto shalt thou come, but no farther; and here shall thy proud waves be stayed."

How far like processes may have advanced in other planets of our own or other systems, it is useless to conjecture. Doubtless infinite variety marks the universe of God; and the phenomena with which we are familiar may or may not characterize the numberless worlds which people space. The great work was advancing; each step in this advance distinctly leading to the accomplishment of the final grand object,—the preparation of a fit abode for sentient beings. Thus far God had exerted His power in the operation of mighty laws over insensate matter. All was completed, and "God said, Let the earth bring forth;" and, lo! life, mysterious, incomprehensible principle, in its earliest, primitive manifestation, burst upon the universe. Earth's teeming womb heaved, and up sprang the waving grass, the tender flower, the shoot, the shrub, the tree. Earth, enrobed in her glorious livery, shook her ten thousand leaves, flashed back the golden hue of fruit and flower, breathed the incense of her spicy groves, in grateful offerings to the living God.

Such is the record. So Moses hath written, that on the third day, before the sun was, God commanded the earth to bring forth, and grass, and herb, and tree, each yielding seed in its kind, covered the earth's surface. Here three inquiries present themselves. First, does the order of geological strata concur with the nebular theory? Do the fossil remains of vegetables occupy a location consistent with their announced primitive creation? and, finally, how are we to account for the existence of vegetable life while there is no sun.

It is not my intention, as it is not my province, to enter into a detailed discussion of each of these questions. If we assign to our globe a nebulous origin, its solidification would be the consequence of radiation of heat. A cooling down of the exterior would allow the gradual approach of the particles, until, finally, chemical laws begin their action, crystallization follows, and certain forms of the granitic rocks are produced. It is enough that eminent geologists have advocated that the great phenomena of the primitive formations not only possibly, but probably, agree with the hypothesis of igneous origin.

What, then, is the testimony with regard to the first forms of organic life on earth? The most than can be derived from the explorations of geology, is the conclusion that the introduction of animal and vegetable life was contemporaneous. This is but negative testimony, and only demonstrates the fact, that no vegetable remains have been preserved which grew prior to the introduction of animal life on earth. The record, then, is left unbroken, and it yet remains to be seen whether the more profound researches in progress may not, at some future period, upturn the rocky remains of the primeval vegetation, revealed in the Mosaic record.

The third inquiry is kindred to some already entertained. How could vegetable life exist upon the earth, when as yet there was no sun to fructify and animate the world? I again urge that the objection against the truth of this record, grounded on these facts, proves too much. It was quite as well known to Moses three thousand five hundred years ago, as to ourselves, that without the light and heat of the sun no vegetation can exist, and in case the writer had been composing a theory of creation, merely from his own human investigation and research, he never would have committed so gross a blunder as to people earth with fruit and flower, before he had first formed and fashioned the great central source of all life, and light, and heat.

There is a deeper meaning in this narrative,

and in case we admit the nebulous origin of our planet, and the order of development incident to this hypothesis, we perceive at once that all difficulty vanishes with reference to the sustentation of animal and vegetable life, previous to the fourth grand era, when the sun, and moon, and stars, were to burst forth in all their magnificence and beauty.

There was light in abundance though the great source of light was as yet vailed in a misty shroud which no eye could have pierced had eye then existed.

The uncondensed and unlimited atmospheric envelope, which in the third grand epoch, enshrouded sun and moon, and hid the forming stars, did not forbid the penetration of light and heat. Besides, the central heat of our globe in itself, formed in the primitive ages a source of vegetable activity when God had once called vegetation into existence, which must have stimulated the primeval forests to the most vigorous and luxurious development. Such, indeed, is the fact, and hence we find species of gigantic dimensions among the ruins of those early ages, whose existing types are so diminutive as scarcely to be recognized of the same family.

Thus it would seem that in this third grand era, the order of creation is in strict accordance with the determinate truths of science, and are only to be explained and rendered intelligible, by resort to the theory of the nebulous origin of our planet.

It should ever be borne carefully in mind, that all we have said is but an attempted interpretation. This may be entirely wrong and utterly false, while the Mosaic record shall remain eternal as truth itself. We interpret by the light of existent science. What new beams may be hereafter kindled no one will venture to predict, and what wonderful modifications of interpretation may be presented in the light of these new fires, it is equally impossible to divine.

We have now reached the fourth grand epoch in the formation of the universe. "And God said, Let there be lights in the firmament of the heavens to divide the day from the night, and let them be for signs and for seasons, and for days and for years; and let them be for lights in the firmament of the heaven, to give light upon the earth, and it was so. And God made two great lights; the greater light to rule the day, and the lesser light to rule the night; He made the stars also; and God set them in the firmament of the heaven to give light upon the earth, and to rule over the day and over the night, and to divide the light from the darkness, and God saw that it was good."

We have already adverted to our explanation of the prominent fact proclaimed in this passage. The formation of the sun, moon, and planets, on the fourth day of creation. In case we admit the origin proposed in our foregoing examinations, we will readily understand that many ages would roll away, even after the commenced formation of the solar system, before the sun, or moon, or stars, would either hold their present form or exhibit their present appearance. Moses was not commissioned to reveal the details of scientific truth, but simply to present the grand outlines and order of progressive creation or development. He declares then simply that before the sun, and moon, and stars, as they now exist were formed, certain antecedent events had occurred. These were the creation of matter; the enactment of physical laws; the generation of light; the formation of an expanse, by the aggregation of matter, around appointed centers; the final consolidation of our earth; the emergence of its lands and continents from the primeval seas; the clothing of earth with vegetable life. Such are the facts announced as existent prior to the formation of the sun, moon, and stars, as we now see them. We interpret, moreover, Moses to say, that three vast periods of time, denominated "days," had already passed away, and now the question arises, may all these events have preceded the present physical constitution of sun, moon, and stars. We are disposed to answer this question in the affirmative and without hesitation, and even to assert that this is the precise order of nature, in case the nebular theory be the true cosmogony of the universe.

It is useless to go into extensive details after what we have already said; I will remark, however, that our earth is one of the smallest of all the planets. It was thrown from the sun's equator a long time after the outer planets, and at a time when a comparative condensation of the sun's matter had been reached. Being small, it would lose its caloric with great rapidity, and would cool down far more rapidly than the larger planets, and almost infinitely faster than the sun. It would, therefore, become a fit theater for vegetable existence, long before the sun would lose its nebulosity, a part of which even yet remains, and long before its own atmosphere had become sufficiently translucent to permit the sun, or moon, or stars, to be seen, even had they existed in their present well-defined and brilliant forms.

We perceive, therefore, that it was not until all the events above narrated had occurred, that it could be said that God placed two great lights in the firmament to rule the day, and to divide between the day and the night, and to be for signs and for seasons and for days and for years. Previous to this period, they could have served none of these ends; they were not great lights any more than they now are when our atmosphere, dense with vapor, renders them invisible; they did not divide distinctly between the day and the night; no one could have distinguished, at the first opening of human eye on the then existent world, whether it was day or night; a dim, nebulous haze pervaded the earth, —a sort of luminous fog, such as now visits us, and renders it impossible to distinguish the light of a concealed moon from the coming of day. There was no sunrise visibly distinct, even if mortal eye had existed to see it. There was, in like manner, no sunset. Day and night, though severed, were not separable. They were intermingled; it was, or would have been, impossible for us to have pronounced where the one ended and the other commenced. But this condition of things had now reached its termination. The atmosphere had been gradually becoming transparent; the sun had been condensing; the moon had, in like manner, gradually assumed her definite outlines; and, finally, a purity of the ethereal regions and of the earth's atmosphere was gained,—such that two great lights shone forth in the heavens, to divide the day from the night, and the stars also glittered in the blue vault.

Previous to this condition of nature, neither the sun, moon, nor stars could be said to give their light upon the earth as they now give it. More especially was it impossible for these celestial orbs to fill for man one great end of their being and organization. Mark well the language:—They were given for signs and for seasons, and for days and for years. They were to give their light upon the earth. Previous to this epoch they could neither be for signs nor seasons, nor for days, nor months, nor years; they could not give their light on the earth in the individual, specific sense in which it is now given.

There are those who find in this narrative of the formation of sun, moon, and stars, and the appointment of their functions with reference to our earth, an extravagant prominence of so small a planet as our earth, and a sort of degradation of these great celestial orbs, in making them in any sense tributary to the earth. But if any one will attempt to modify the record of Moses, so as to avoid any appearance of subordination of the sun, moon, and stars to the earth, and yet to retain a distinct statement of the uses of these celestial orbs, the task will be found far more difficult than it appears at first view. Let it be remembered that no distinct revelation of astronomical facts was intended. Moses was not to declare the relative magnitude of the sun and moon, and earth and stars; he was not to reveal the functions of these bodies with reference to other planets; it was only in relation to the earth that their characteristics were to be presented. These bodies do sustain the very relations to the earth announced by Moses. The sun and moon are two great lights, which rule over the day and the night, and the stars shed their light upon the earth. Let us go back in imagination to the condition of things during the preceding eras in the earth's history. Let us people the earth with intelligent beings, organized like ourselves, at the time when neither sun, nor moon, nor stars were visible,— when there was no distinct separation between day and night,—when the impenetrable atmospheric veil, like the present clouds of earth, shut out forever the sun, moon, and stars. What would have been man's condition on such an earth? The climate might have been never so pure and genial; perpetual spring might have spread its beauties over the virgin earth; fruit, and flower, and the ripened corn and the clustering grape might have wooed the hand of man; the earth might have spread upon her surface every thing to enchant the eye, or gratify the taste, or satiate the appetite, and yet man would have lived in a dimly-illumined prison. The earth alone would have been his universe. How could he have risen to any knowledge of the glories of God? Could he ever have surmised even the actual condition of the planet he inhabited? All would have been a twilight far more deep and sombre to his intellect than that natural gloom which surrounded his physical frame. How wonderful would have been the change to such inhabitants of earth, when the sun burst forth for the first time and flooded the earth with light! when the moon, throned among her shining stars, assumed her reign over the dewy night! when days and months, and seasons and years began to mark the on-going of time! How wonderful a change would this have been, and yet God appointed these specific functions to these mighty orbs, and neither more nor less is asserted by Moses.

It is not asserted that the sun and moon and stars were formed for no other purpose than to give light to the earth. God set them in the firmament, in the expanse, in space, in such positions as to yield their light in quantities adapted to the wants of earth. Their distances were accurately adjusted, they were firmly set in the heavens, so that no derangement could ever occur to deprive the earth of its supply of light, or to flood it with an insufferable blaze.

It is not my province to follow further in detail the order of creation. I have now closed an examination of so much of the Mosaic account as belongs specifically to the science of Astronomy. On the fifth day we are informed that the waters were commanded "to bring forth abundantly every moving creature that hath life, and the fowl that may fly above the earth." On the sixth day the earth was commanded to bring forth " the living creature after his kind, cattle and creeping thing, and every beast of the earth after his kind, and it was so ;" and, finally, after the earth had been clothed with vegetation, after the ocean teemed with its inhabitants, after bird and beast peopled the earth, " God said, Let us make man in our own image, after our own likeness."

Man, then, according to the account of Moses, was only placed upon the earth after all inferior races had been formed. On the third day, or during the third great period, vegetation was brought into being; on the fourth, the sun, moon, and stars broke through the misty shroud that had previously enveloped them; on the fifth day the ocean and air were peopled with their tribes; on the sixth, earth teemed with its flocks and herds; and, finally, man was formed, and God breathed into his nostrils the breath of life, and he became a living soul.

Such is the order of creation in the heavens and on the earth, announced by Moses,—such the multitude of facts asserted in this primitive record,—such the extended outline, vulnerable by science at every point, but as yet entirely unbroken in its whole extent. "Thus the heavens and the earth were finished, and all the host of them." Earth was peopled with its multitudinous tribes, and space floated with the millions of shining orbs which were henceforth to declare the glory of God. The mighty work was ended, and Jehovah rested from His work on the seventh day. As in the work of creation six epochs had been employed, and as God had rested from His work on the commencement of the seventh, so time was now divided, by divine appointment, into weeks of seven days, six of which man should devote to labor and industry, and the seventh to rest and the worship of the one only God.

That the period of time denominated a week is of exceedingly antique origin, is manifest from the fact that its use is found among all the primitive nations of the earth. The Egyptians, Babylonians, Persians, Hindoos, Chinese, Arabians, all employed this arbitrary division of time.

Nations scattered over the surface of the earth, widely separated and without intercourse, have adopted the same, conventionally demonstrating that it must have descended to each from some common origin.

I do not perceive, then, that a valid objection can be urged against the long periods by which the word "day" is interpreted, in consequence of the institution of the sabbath.

I place myself in the attitude of one disposed to cavil at the claims of the Bible, and when I see so curious, so unexpected, so astonishing a parallelism between the facts of the Mosaic record and those which are evolved on the present most probable scientific hypotheses; when I reflect that the division of time now in use is to be traced back to a period far beyond the reach of history, I do not feel that an interpretation, which has about it so much the air of truth and probability, can be shaken by an objection based upon the institution of the sabbath of rest.

Let us look for some higher, some more positive proof of the human origin of this strange book. Surely, if it be the composition of mere man, and of many men, we shall find it deficient in some department of science. For the present, then, let us abandon this objection, in case more powerful ones can be urged, and should we find this to be the only one, we may abandon it with the greater safety.

Such is the exposition and interpretation which we are disposed to put upon this Scriptural account, of the great operation of creation. It may be defective, it may be even radically wrong. The nebular hypothesis itself may be superseded by some other theory entirely different, when more light shall be shed upon this account, and its truth or falsehood may be forever irrevocably fixed. What may come we know not, until science shall reveal a true cosmogony; until science shall have fixed on a basis of truth strong and immovable her assertions with reference to this great event, a final positive investigation will be impossible. This entire account must be viewed in the light of a prophetic declaration, which, unfulfilled, no one can with certainty interpret, but the moment the accomplishment has taken place, then a blaze of light is thrown upon every line of the prophetic announcement, and it is all instinct with light and truth. Such, doubtless, will be the case with reference to the Mosaic account of creation. If it be the dictation of the ever-living God, then in His own time He will permit the human mind to rise higher and still higher in its researches in the universe, until, God aiding, it shall reach, by its own struggles, to the knowledge of the plan by which this world we inhabit, these planets that roll and shine, and yonder sun, luminiferous and resplendent with all the host of Heaven, were brought to people the unlimited regions of vacuity.

In the mean time, let us bring to the test of exact scientific examination those passages which may be scattered through this volume, and learn the result of this critical scrutiny.

LECTURE V.

AN EXAMINATION OF THE ASTRONOMICAL ALLUSIONS
IN THE BOOK OF JOB

LECTURE V.

AN EXAMINATION OF THE ASTRONOMICAL ALLUSIONS IN
THE BOOK OF JOB.

THE authorship of this remarkable book seems not to be clearly settled. All are, however, agreed in assigning to it the highest antiquity. Although the incidents recorded are of the most astonishing character, its claims to its place in the sacred canon remains undisputed. With a short introduction in prose, and a still shorter close, this book is a poem of the highest order. We are not, however, concerned with its poetry, or with the style or nature of the composition; we are not called upon to discuss its beautiful imagery or its exquisite language;—it is only in its incidental and wonderful use of certain grand phenomena of nature that we claim a special interest. A controversy between Job and his three friends occupies a large proportion of the poem; the arguments are finally summed up by a fifth individual, Elihu, when Jehovah's voice is heard out of the whirlwind pronouncing judgment.

It is within the limits of this part of the poem that we find a series of questions propounded, having for their specific object the utter overthrow and humiliation of the feeble judgment of man. When we consider the age in which this book must have been composed, and the utter impossibility that any knowledge of the true system of the universe then obtained, we shall be compelled to acknowledge the exceeding difficulty of propounding, at that early day, any series of astronomical inquiries which could be put, at the present day, with equal certainty of accomplishing the object designed by these interrogatories.

This may not be so readily granted by some: first, because they may contend for a very high state of intelligence among the primitive nations in astronomical science; and, second, because it may be by some asserted that it is by no means difficult for the ignorant to propound queries which the wise can not answer.

I have examined with some care the attainments of the early nations in astronomy. Almost nothing has come down to us directly from the primitive nations; but as the Greek philosophers traveled extensively among the Egyptians, the Babylonians, and Hindoos, we may confidently assert that little important knowledge could have been concealed from these earnest and devoted seekers after knowledge.

Should we even admit the claims to authenticity of the most remote observations even upon the heliacal rising of the stars upon eclipses, and upon the conjunctions which are contended for by the most ardent devotees to the antique in science, we shall scarcely go back, in any one of these simple astronomical observations, to the age in which this poem was composed. It bears within it evidence (as we shall presently see) of high antiquity. If, then, the Greek philosophers could draw almost nothing from these imagined treasures of early knowledge,—if the crude notions and reasonings of Pythagoras are fair specimens of the ideas entertained by the primitive nations among whom he studied, we certainly can not claim any real knowledge of the true system of the universe for so high an antiquity. We do not think it possible that any such knowledge could have been lost, if ever reached by any of the ancient nations. The Hindoos claim, in common with the Egyptians and Babylonians, a very high antiquity. These claims we propose to consider hereafter. While they urge these claims to be of high antiquity, one thing is certain, they urge no claims to superior knowledge of the system of nature. The very crudest notions were entertained with reference to the most striking phenomena, and a manifest ignorance prevailed with reference to their true cause and interpretation.

It is, I think, impossible, then, to affirm that, in the age to which we must assign the composition of this poem, any such knowledge of the order, and laws, and phenomena of nature, and of our system, prevailed as would have served to guide him who attempted to propound a series of deep and difficult questions. With regard to the second objection, that an ignorant person may ask questions which great wisdom can not answer,—while we admit the force of the truism, we do not think it applicable to the present case. We affirm that a positive evidence of the amount of knowledge which any one possesses of any subject, will be perfectly evinced by the following test: give to the person under examination an extended series of questions relating to the science professed, and bid him select the most difficult from the printed catalogue; accident may aid him for one or two questions, but admitting him to be ignorant of the answers to all the questions, they are all equally difficult to him, and, of course, on this hypothesis any selection would inevitably betray his ignorance, and should he succeed in making a selection truly involving the most difficult inquiries (he being ignorant), it could only be accounted for by the intervention of divine aid.

If we admit, then, that the Book of Job was composed in an age of the world when all were ignorant of the true system of the universe, and if within its compass we should find a series of astronomical inquiries, professedly selected and put to overwhelm the human mind, in case these same inquiries, at this day and in the full blaze of science, and with all our knowledge of the system of nature, should be equally overwhelming, we should in reason acknowledge that they could not have been propounded by human ignorance, and must have proceeded, as is professed, from the mouth of Him who built the universe, and to whom all secrets were open as the face of day.

With these preliminary remarks, we proceed to examine the subject with all humility and candor. " Then the Lord answered Job out of the whirlwind, and said, *Who is this that darkeneth counsel by words without knowledge?*" One of the most sublime sentences that ever was penned! Who is this that *darkeneth* counsel by *words* without *knowledge?* Who is this who pretends to call in question the justice of the government of Jehovah? Is God to be arraigned by worms of the dust? by beings whose profoundest wisdom is but darkness, whose efforts to elucidate but spread a deeper darkness? " Gird up now thy loins like a man; for I will demand of thee, and answer thou me." If, indeed, ye are competent to sit in judgment on the acts of God, then surely your wisdom must have taught you the grand secrets of nature. "Where wast thou when I laid the foundations of the earth? declare, if thou hast understanding. Who hath laid the measures thereof, if thou knowest; or who hath stretched the line upon it? Whereupon are the foundations thereof fastened; or who hath laid the cornerstone thereof? When the morning stars sang together, and all the sons of God shouted for joy?"

Could the astonished Job, or his still more astonished opponents, make any response to these humiliating questions? Has there ever been a time, following down the thousands of years which have elapsed even to the present moment, when all the accumulated wisdom of man could make any reply?

Some may object to this passage, and urge that it actually intimates an ignorance of the true condition of the earth by the interrogation, otherwise the word "foundations" would not have been used. To this objection let me answer that the Hebrew word translated "foundations" means really sockets, something whereon a pivot turns; and the word translated "fastened" is better rendered, "made to sink," as though the question had been put, in case this earth is fixed, and the heavens revolve about it whereon are the sockets made to sink, of the axis of this revolution? or if the earth itself rotates, tell me how are the sockets fastened by which it is sustained?

If this should appear to any one an overstrained paraphrase or translation,—if it still be asserted that there is not in the passage sufficient ground for such an interpretation, I must beg the common privilege of all interpreters to explain the difficult and doubtful passages of this book by others from the same book throwing light upon the same subject. If it still be asserted that the word "foundations" is to be considered as referring to the vulgar notion that the earth was fixed on some unknown support, by which it was buoyed up, I must quote a single sentence, as beautiful as it is wonderful, which will place forever this matter at rest. In another part of this poem, when acknowledging the majesty and power of God, Job declares that "He" (God) "stretcheth out the north over the empty place, and hangeth the earth upon nothing." How astonishing is this declaration! God stretcheth out the north over vacuity, over immensity. Deep sunk in space, away in the remote north, in the region of vacuity, was seen that point about which either the heavens or the earth revolved. But the earth itself *hangeth on nothing*. It is suspended in space; there are no foundations; and who can tell whereon are fastened the sockets of its rotation?

Let us come, then, to the answer to this question. Propound it to the modern astronomer, to the geometer of the present age. Whereupon is the earth hung in empty space, and where is fastened the socket on which its firm axle is fixed? Shall it be answered that the earth is linked to the great center by the power of universal gravitation? What, I demand, is this potent energy which has been named gravitation. Wherein is this power lodged? Who hath ever grasped it in his hand, or seen, or heard, or felt it? Not one. Let us not mistake—gravitation is but a name; it is the representation of a vast multitude of phenomena, witnessed in the heavens and upon the earth, attributable to a cause always acting according to an invariable law,—and we call this gravitation. No one has ever conceived what it is, —no one, probably, ever will conceive what it may be; and all we can say is this, that the great First Cause is pleased to manifest His power in the guidance of the orbs of heaven according to one uniform law established by Himself, and to a knowledge of that law of operation man has been permitted to reach;—and here he stops. Not an inch beyond can he advance; and with all his present knowledge,—and I admit it to be great,—he can not answer the question, Whereon are the sockets of the earth fastened, and by whom were they fixed, when God stretched out the north over the empty space, and hung the solid globe, with all its millions, its forests, and oceans, and mountains, upon nothing? When the morning stars sang together, and all the sons of God shouted for joy?

It may still be urged that no inquiry, with reference to the earth, could be made which could be answered; that they are all equally difficult and equally unanswerable, if taken in the broad sense we have claimed for the foregoing inquiry. I answer that this is not the case. Suppose it had been asked,—Knowest thou the form of the earth on which thou dwellest? Canst thou comprehend its mighty outlines by thy tiny measures? Hast thou weighed it in a balance and computed its dimensions? Each of these questions, in my opinion, would have been just as unanswerable by Job or his friends as those actually put; while to the modern astronomer their approximate answer at least would present no difficulty, and we should at this day have regarded such questions as proof positive that the interrogator was only proposing questions which he could not himself answer.

This first question which we have considered regarded the solid earth. We now come to the examination of the second interrogation : " Or who shut up the sea with doors when it broke forth, as if it had issued out of the womb? when I made the cloud the garment thereof, and thick darkness a swaddling-band for it, and broke up for it my decreed place, and set bars and doors, and said, Hitherto shalt thou come, but no farther; and here shall thy proud waves be stayed?"

I must be permitted here to remark, once for all, that it is in these and kindred passages that the greatest difficulty has been found by translators. This will be readily appreciated when we reflect how difficult it is for us to comprehend a work written even in our own language that refers to matters of science of which we are ignorant. The difficulty is increased, in an enormous ratio, if we be attempting to translate a foreign tongue, and the matters treated of are such as we could not comprehend, even if written in our own language. Such was the difficulty encountered by the translators of the Bible in all those cases involving a reference to scientific matters, of which not only themselves but the age in which they lived were ignorant. It was even worse than this. False notions were entertained, to accord with which, in many instances, there was a disposition to bend the sense of the original, to make it, as was supposed, the more intelligible.

In this interrogation the passage translated, " and brake up for it my decreed place," is properly rendered, " established my decree upon it;" that is, upon the ocean; a decree by which it should be forever governed. No one, who has considered the problem of the stability of the ocean, can fail to recognize the depth and difficulty of the inquiry here propounded. Look at this mighty mass of waters, covering more than two thirds of the entire surface of the globe, subject to the influence of the fierce and resistless tornado, wrought up into tumultuous confusion, its waves rolling and dashing against the clouds, and lashing with fury the resounding shore. Where, I ask, is the guarantee that whole continents shall not be submerged, and every vestige of life swept from the surface of the earth?

How wonderful are the adjustments by which the ocean is fixed within the limits assigned by the decree of Omnipotence! Let us point out some of those conditions without which no stability could exist. If it were possible to empty the waters of earth's oceans into the cavities which probably diversify the surface of the planet Saturn, and thus spread over its surface the heavy ocean of earth, so long as all was tranquil the waves would sleep, and a placid ocean would spread its unbroken sheet from shore to shore. But now let loose upon its surface the mighty force of those winds which stir its profoundest depths on earth, and no precipitous shore, no mountain barrier, could restrain the swelling billow; it would heave, and dash, and rise, till, finally, breaking every barrier, it would engulf island and continent, and chaos would assert its ancient empire.

How is it, then, that the ocean on earth is shut up with bars and doors, while, if removed to Saturn, no decree of earth can bind it? It is due to the fact that there exists a nice adjustment of the relative specific gravity of the solid earth and the fluid wave, and of the gaseous atmosphere. The earth greatly preponderates over the gravity of the ocean, and the ocean vastly preponderates over the gravity of the air. If our ocean were removed to Saturn, this fluid, unstable covering would possess a greater specific gravity than the solid body of the planet, and it would be like a globe of cork swimming in an envelop of water. The least cause of derangement would cause the waters to rush to one side of the planet, and the globe would, in some sense, float on this concentrated abyss of waters, to be tossed and rolled over and over, and every portion submerged at any and every moment. Such would be the condition of the earth were the relative specific gravities of the earth, air, and water changed.

But the power of the atmosphere is not the only force which disturbs the tranquillity of the ocean wave. All are familiar with the phenomenon of the tides; those wonderful heavings of the mass of waters which are periodical, and are due to the powerful influence of the moon and sun. We know that astonishing variations in the heights of the tidal waves occur at different epochs, and why may it not happen that by some dire conjunction of conspiring influences, this mighty wave shall not overleap the appointed barriers, and submerge the earth? Here, again, the conditions of equilibrium are as wonderful as they are complicated. What will be thought when I tell you that this stability of the ocean involves nothing less than the organization of the entire solar system! Each one of the worlds constituting this stupendous system has its part to play in maintaining the decree which God has established upon the ocean. At one period in the history of astronomy it seemed that the decree of God must one day be violated. The moon has been slowly approaching the earth from the earliest ages of the world. From this approach the tides due to her influence are now heaved up to a greater height than they were four thousand years ago. Should this decrease in the moon's distance continue, the time must come when the tide, rising superior to every barrier, would whelm the earth, and God's decree, "Hitherto shalt thou come, and no farther; and here shall thy proud waves be stayed," become null, and the declaration of this so-called sacred volume would be falsified. But science, after a long and arduous struggle, at length discovered the fact that this decrease of the moon's distance, due to the planetary disturbance of the figure of the earth's orbit, had its limits fixed quite as positively as those by which God has declared He would restrain the ocean. The time will come when the decrease of distance is changed into an increase, and the moon slowly leaves the earth by the same degrees by which it had, for hundreds of thousands of years, made its approach, and with it sinks the crest of the heaving tide; and thus do ocean wave and rolling moon rise and roll, and heave and shine in precise accordance, each subject to the will of God, who hath in wisdom fixed the boundary of their movements.

It is certainly sufficiently wonderful that the height of the ocean wave should be dependent on the relative magnitudes, distances, and specific gravities of the sun, earth, moon, and planets. No one of these could be altered or interchanged and yet leave the ocean's stability unaffected. But there is a still more astonishing condition of stability dependent on the figure of the earth and its velocity of rotation on its axis. As this is referred to in the next interrogatory, we will discuss it in that connection.

God further demands of Job: "Hast thou commanded the morning since thy days, and caused the day-spring from on high to know his place? * * * That it might take hold of the ends of the earth. * * * It is turned as clay to the seal, and they stand as a garment." Portions of this passage are exceedingly obscure, as now translated. It seems manifest that reference is made to the admirable order of recurrence of day and night, and the beautiful adjustments by which the dawn breaks quietly upon a slumbering world. Hast thou commanded the coming of morning since thy days, or hast thou taught the day-spring from on high to know his place? Is it at thy bidding, or in accordance with thy will, that the solid earth spins swiftly on its axle, and with such an unchanging motion that the morning never fails, that the sun knoweth his going down, and the day-spring his appointed place?

To the casual reader little may seem to be implied in these profound and overwhelming interrogatories; but to him who reads aright, and in the full meridian light of modern science, there is such a power and dignity and majesty in these questions, that the human mind, proud as it is by nature, sinks in low abasement, and acknowledges its utter weakness, its absolute littleness.

God demands who launched this globe in space, who set bars and doors to the heaving deep, and who maintains its swift rotation, by which all nature is hastened, and without which life would become extinct and animation die. Can man accomplish these grand designs by which his very being is maintained? God can live though nature die; while man sinks and perishes with any and every change, and yet he is impotent to maintain a single phenomenon by which he lives.

With how much precision has the day-spring from on high been taught to know his place! For more than three thousand years science has gone backward, and, with profound research, reveals the fact that in that vast period the length of the day has not changed by the hundredth part of a single second of time. No matter how numerous the causes of change, how diversified in their action, how multiplied in their effects, out of them comes an admirable equilibrium, and the earth, with undying velocity, spins on its sleeping axle.

Go to him who, night after night, watches the revolving heavens; mark with what implicit confidence he relies on the mighty truth that God has taught the day-spring from on high to know his place. He takes his position to signalize the meridian passage of his star,—on the preceding night it had passed at such a moment of time marked on the face of his clock, and again to night at the same hour, minute, and second, and even to the very thousandth of a second, true to the bidding of an unchanging Will, his telescope, borne by the revolving earth, glances the visual ray to the very center of the same identical star! Nothing can exceed the absolute uniformity of the earth's rotation. This is not the attribute of celestial motion generally.

The earth, in its annual orbitual motion, is perpetually changing its velocity. The moon, in like manner, moves at an irregular pace; and every planet—and more especially the comets—exhibit extraordinary changes of velocity. Why is it that the rotation of the earth on its axis should be maintained? Should we not expect that, in the lapse of thousands of years, this rotation would slowly die away and disappear? How can it be maintained with such absolute perfection? Again we are lost; again we are driven for explanation to Divine energy. God hath commanded the morning, and taught the dayspring to know his place. But, it may be demanded, wherein lies the necessity of this uniformity of motion? Could not the earth quite as well have fulfilled its functions without this nice and beautiful adjustment? The answer is in the negative. From the rotation of the earth we derive our unit of time. By means of its uniformity we are permitted the more conveniently to investigate the movements of the celestial orbs, and to reach to a knowledge of the great mysteries of creation.

Let this velocity decay by never so small an amount, and soon the temperature of the earth's various regions becomes deranged, disorder enters every kingdom of nature, and, finally, destruction ensues. Let the velocity be increased by never so small a constant increment, and a like result necessarily ensues. But, more astonishing still, any change of the velocity of rotation would disturb the equilibrium of the ocean, and cause it to pass the barriers which God has assigned to limit its heaving waves.

This fact is distinctly alluded to, and in the most emphatic language, in this same most remarkable poem.

But, it may be asked, what has the rotation of the earth on its axis to do with the retention of the sea within its bounds? Let me briefly explain. Were the earth at rest, its figure, if even globular, might have maintained its exact spherical form. The moment, however, that rotation on an axis commences, the equilibrium is disturbed, a new force (the centrifugal) is introduced, and a modification of the earth's form necessarily follows. Hence we find the earth protuberant at the equator and flattened at the poles, simply because at the equatorial regions the velocity of the particles being a maximum, the resulting centrifugal force is the greatest, and the earth is therefore evolved at its equator far above the level which would exist were it at rest. There is an immense equatorial belt surrounding the equator, like an immense continuous mountain, upon whose sloping sides the equatorial oceans are maintained, not by gravity alone, but by the action of that force which is dependent on the velocity of the earth's rotation on its axis. Could we grasp the solid earth, and even by slow degrees arrest its rotatory motion, a universal deluge would be the consequence. The water would overleap all opposing barriers and flow with rushing speed to the poles, while an enormous continent of dry land would emerge from the deep and surround the equator of the earth. With a full knowledge of these facts, understanding clearly that the day and the night result, in their continuity and perfection, from the uniformity of the earth's rotation, and that from the same cause the ocean itself is restrained within the limits assigned by God, how powerful does the declaration sound, powerful only because of its exact truth, *"He hath compassed the waters with bounds, until the day and the night shall come to an end."* How strange it is, that in case the day and the night should come to an end, should the earth cease to roll on its well-poised axis, then God hath no longer compassed the waters with bounds; the boundaries are overleaped; and old ocean, released from its fetters, invades the dry land, and desolation follows its terrible march through the earth.

It is in vain to urge that the expression, "until the day and the night shall come to an end," simply means that God has compassed the waters with bounds until the end of time. This double sense of these wonderful expressions is found too often recurring to be the result of accident. The language appears to be selected to be at all times appropriate, and to grow brighter and more luminous as science shall shed upon it a brighter glow.

How many questions might have been propounded, with reference to the earth and ocean, which would have only betrayed the ignorance of the interrogator? Had it been demanded whether Job had ever sounded the depths of the mighty deep,—had he ever traversed its boundless extent? Could he declare the secrets which were hidden on its unknown shores? These queries might have served to overwhelm the mind of God's ancient patriarch, but at present they would have lost their force. How absurd does the following declaration of Hesiod, descriptive of the earth's position between heaven and Tartarus:

"From the high heaven a brazen anvil cast,
Nine days and nights in rapid whirls would last,
And reach the earth the tenth; whence strongly hurled
The same the passage to th' infernal world."

I say how absurd does this declaration appear now, when we know that for a body to fall even from the sun (whose distance is almost an insensible quantity compared with that of the stars of heaven), it would require no less than sixty-four days and a half; and from the fixed stars, instead of nine days, as asserted by the Greek poet, it would require more than forty-two millions of days! In case we should find such crude statements within the limits of the sacred volume put forth as substantial truth, our faith in its origin would end, and its sacred character would be destroyed forever.

We return to the passage under consideration. We have seen how much power and meaning there is in the question, "Hast thou commanded the morning since thy days?" But how are we to interpret the words of the context: "And caused the day-spring from on high to know his place; that it might take hold of the ends of the earth. It is turned as clay to the seal, and they stand as a garment." This, I take it, refers to the beautiful provision for lighting up the world by slow and progressive degrees. Why is it that we do not pass instantly from the deep gloom of midnight darkness to the full blaze of noonday? Not because it requires the earth twelve hours to rotate from midnight to noon. There is a far different reason. Who has never watched with delight the first faint evidence of the coming day? A feeble uncertain glow lights up the eastern heavens, this slowly brightening, the upper air flings down the rays of the coming sun. The ruddy glow deepens, a crimson hue suffuses the east, until at length the first ray of the sun darts with gentle splendor upon the earth. Slowly this orb heaves up his stupendous disc, yet shorn of half his beams by the thirsty atmosphere drenched with his glorious hues.

Here, again, we find evidence of the goodness and wisdom of God. Such is the constitution of light, and such the property of the atmosphere, that by means of the latter the direction of the former is bent from its track, curved round the earth and moulded to its form as the clay to the seal, and standing about the earth as a resplendent garment of light. Such at least is the interpretation which these difficult passages seem to admit. It may be proper to remark, that the word translated "ends" of the earth is more literally rendered "wings," as though allusion were made to the atmosphere as a sort of wings outstretched around the body of the earth.

God yet further interrogates Job: "Hast thou perceived the breadth of the earth; declare if thou knowest it all?" Here it would seem we have at length found one interrogatory which, although Job could not answer it, is now readily answered. Do we not know the extent of the earth? Has not man circumnavigated its surface? Has he not perceived it all? It is true we have sailed round the earth, but it is equally true, that in its breadth, its latitude (for this is the meaning, as would appear from the ancient usage, of length and breadth as applied to the earth), no one has yet perceived or actually suspected the breadth of the earth. To do this we must go from pole to pole, to compass the earth's breadth or latitude. We must penetrate these hyperborean regions, the empire of eternal frost, in which the secrets of the north as well as of the south appears to be forever locked. It is then equally impossible now and will be a thousand years hence, as it was three thousand years ago, for man to declare that he has actually perceived with his own eyes the entire breadth or latitude of the earth.

Here, again, some may say that this is special interpretation. The only reply to be made is, that it fairly admits this explanation, and to this advantage the advocate of the inspired volume is justly entitled.

Again the Almighty demands of Job, "Where is the way where light dwelleth, and as for darkness, where is the place thereof, that thou shouldst take it to the bounds thereof, and that thou shouldst know the paths to the house thereof? Knowest thou it because thou wert then born, or because the number of thy days is great?" Here we are presented with a series of inquiries of the most astonishing character. The dwelling-place of light and of darkness. The bounds of each. The paths to the house of light. Did Job comprehend these mysteries, and if so was it because he was then born and because the number of his days was great? How strange and unintelligible these queries, and why does the knowledge of them imply an age the number of whose days is great?

Who shall answer these profound inquiries? Who shall declare to us the character of light?

What is this wondrous phenomenon known to us under the name of light? Is it a modification of matter, shot forever with incredible velocity from heaven's blazing orbs: anon pure and white, and then flashing with every imaginable color? If it be particles of matter, infinitesimal globules, how comes it that the most delicate organ of the human frame, the eye, is not torn, and wounded, and lacerated, by the millions of particles which fall upon its surface? Is light the effect of vibrations of our ethereal medium, pervading all space, almost infinitely elastic, and darting its waves from the center to the circumference like thought? Then how wonderful the reflection that only certain bodies possess the property of giving to this medium the velocity of undulation demanded for the propagation and production of light. Where is the way where light dwelleth? Is its home in the sun and stars? Does it inhabit the ether which filleth immensity, or is it by some inscrutable provision of nature made to dwell in that wonderful optical instrument the eye? One thing we know, without it and without the eye all nature were a blank; the heavens vanish; earth's flowers fade, and darkness wraps the globe.

But knowest thou the paths to the house thereof? Hast thou traced the flashing fluid to the bounds thereof? Canst thou say that here is the limit beyond which light has never passed, and, gazing into the dark abyss beyond, declare there darkness reigns? How deep and stupendous these questions to him who hath attempted, with "optic tube," to fathom the deep profound of God's glorious universe.

Go with me to yonder "light-house of the skies." Poised on its rocky base, behold that wondrous tube which lifts the broad pupil of its eye high up as if gazing instinctively into the mighty deep of space. Look out upon the heavens, and gather into your eye its glittering constellations. Pause and reflect that over the narrow zone of the retina of your eye a universe is pictured, painted by light in all its exquisite and beautiful proportions. Look upon that luminous zone which girdles the sky,—observe its faint and cloudy light. How long, think you, that light has been streaming, day and night, with a swiftness which flashes it on its way twelve millions of miles in each and every minute ?—how long has it fled and flashed through space to reach your eye and tell its wondrous tale ? Not less than a century has rolled away since it left its home! Hast thou taken it at the bound thereof? Is this the bound,—here the limit from beyond which light can never come ? Look to yonder point in space, and declare that thou beholdest nothing, absolutely nothing; all is blank and deep and dark. You exclaim, Surely no ray illumines that deep profound. Place your eye for one moment to the tube that now pierces that seeming domain of night, and, lo ! ten thousand orbs, blazing with light unutterable, burst on the astonished sight. Whence start these hidden suns ? Whence comes this light from out deep darkness ? Knowest thou, O man! the paths to the house thereof? Ten thousand years have rolled away since these wondrous beams set out on their mighty journey ! Then you exclaim, We have found the boundary of light; surely none can lie beyond this stupendous limit : far in the deep beyond darkness unfathomable reigns. Look once more. The vision changes; a hazy cloud of light now fills the field of the telescope. Whence comes the light of this mysterious object? Its home is in the mighty deep, as far beyond the limit you had vainly fixed,—ten thousand times as far,—as that limit is beyond the reach of human vision. And thus we mount, and rise, and soar, from height to height, upward, and even upward still, till the mighty series ends, because vision fails, and sinks, and dies.

Hast thou then pierced the boundary of light? Hast thou penetrated the domain of darkness? Hast thou, weak mortal, soared to the fountain whence come these wondrous streams, and taken the light at the hand thereof? Knowest thou the paths to the house thereof? Hast thou stood at yonder infinite origin, and bid that flash depart and journey onward, days, and months, and years; century on century, through countless ages,—millions of years, and never weary in its swift career? Knowest thou when it started? Knowest thou it because thou wast then born, and because the number of thy days is great? Such, then, is the language addressed by Jehovah to weak, erring, mortal man. How has the light of science flooded with meaning this astonishing passage? Surely, surely we do not mis-read,—the interpretation is just.

LECTURE VI.

THE ASTRONOMICAL MIRACLES OF THE BIBLE
MIRACLES OF POWER.

LECTURE VI.

THE ASTRONOMICAL MIRACLES OF THE BIBLE MIRACLES OF POWER.

THE topics which we are about to treat briefly do not fall within the legitimate scope of our investigation. Astronomy has for its object the study and exposition of the phenomena of nature,—not the miracles of God; and hence the uses of astronomy, in illustration, made by the writers of the Hebrew scriptures, may be perfectly in accordance with the exact revelations of modern science, and yet the miraculous accounts stand precisely as we now find them.

It would, therefore, be entirely proper to omit entirely, in our examination of the astronomy of the Bible, any notice of those events which are expressly announced as interpositions of divine power to check and suspend, or even turn back the on-goings of the celestial orbs.

The events to which I allude are the miraculous stopping of the sun and moon for the space of a whole day, at the command of Joshua, and the going backward of the shadow ten degrees on the sun-dial of Ahaz.

I will not undertake to discuss what we are to understand by a miracle, but shall admit, in the outset, that a miraculous event is positively at variance with the established laws of nature, and can only be produced by a power equal to that which enacts and enforces these laws. With this understanding, the first question which presents itself is this :—with our present knowledge of the absolute uniformity of the operation of the laws of nature,—such as the laws of motion and of gravitation,—is it possible to give credence to any statement, no matter how well sustained by human testimony, that in one or more instances these laws have been suspended, and phenomena have occurred directly in opposition to these laws?

It can not be denied that a Power competent to select, enact, and enforce a system of laws, can at His pleasure suspend, alter, or wholly abrogate any or all of them, subject only to this restriction,—that the changes and modifications must be consistent with each other and with what remains. There is no power can accomplish an impossibility—no power can make two and two equal to five; and thus even Omnipotence is compelled to work within limits of definite comprehension.

The physical universe, so far as we understand, is governed by invariable laws. These laws, to a certain extent, have been discovered by human reason and research; and among them none seems to be better established than the laws of motion and gravitation. By these laws the movements of the celestial orbs are controlled; and, so far as human observation extends, there never has been any deviation from these laws.

Is it, then, reasonable or philosophic to accept a statement made in a volume written in an age of the world when these laws governing the physical universe were unknown, which, if credited, compels us to believe that the Creator and sovereign Lawgiver, on two special occasions, suspended, or for a time abrogated these laws as evidence of His good-will to certain of His creatures?

We frankly confess that this subject is surrounded with its difficulties, not so much arising from the abstract question as to whether God can suspend His laws of action, as from the utter ignorance of causes which may operate on the mind of the Supreme to decide that such a suspension should be made. To arrest the sun and moon in mid-heaven to enable one set of combatants to achieve a victory over another, or to turn the sun backward in his career that the shadow on the dial may reverse its movement as a token that God had rebuked the disease under which a Jewish king was suffering, and that fifteen years should be added to his life, are facts which, when presented in their simplest form, are sufficiently incredible. But, unfortunately, human judgment can not by any possibility comprehend the problem. How can a finite being penetrate into the councils of the Infinite? To form a correct judgment in the premises, the mind of man must stretch away down the interminable sweep of time, and trace out to infinitude all the resulting effects and influences in the government of God. In case, then, we admit that circumstances may arise which would render credible a statement that God had interposed, and for a longer or shorter time suspended the laws of nature, we can not fail to perceive that such admission renders it possible to believe, on human testimony, that such an interposition has actually taken place. For we can never know the causes and consequences leading to and resulting from such a miraculous interposition of divine power.

But we may go yet farther and propound the question, Is it reasonable or philosophic, to believe that the Supreme Creator, endowed with omniscience, would originate a scheme of creation and government, wherein invariable laws linked together the entire universe of matter, and then, for any reason, would suspend the operation of these laws for a special purpose, and only with reference to individual objects?

This after all is the great question. It is not whether we are disposed to give credence to one particular alleged miraculous event; but whether it is reasonable to believe that any such event ever did, or ever will take place. I know there are many who deny that a philosopher can believe in a miracle, and yet so far as my limited powers of reasoning can carry me, I am compelled to express the opinion that it is unphilosophic to deny the possibility of miraculous interposition of Divine power.

What are these so-called laws of matter? What are these laws of motion and of gravitation? They are certainly not inherent qualities and properties of matter : if so, this dead insensate matter rises above and superior to the power of God the Creator, and so far as any change in these qualities and properties are concerned, may defy the Omnipotent.

Matter can have no properties, or qualities, or power, except so far as these are derived from the direct and ever-acting will of the Creator. To say, then, that the sun attracts the planets according to the law of gravitation; to say that the planets revolve around the sun in obedience to the laws of motion and gravitation, is nothing more than to say that these material bodies are impelled by the Divine power exerting itself in strict and unalterable harmony with laws which God has chosen, and from which He simply does not choose to deviate.

It may be difficult to conceive and acknowledge that matter possesses of itself no quality, that iron is not hard, lead heavy, water fluid, air gaseous, in and of themselves, and quite independent of even the very being and existence of a Supreme Creator. But how can the particles of iron, or of lead, or of water, or air, exert any force upon each other, which forces, beyond a doubt, operating between the particles of these materials, give to them their outward qualities of hardness, or heaviness, or fluidity. Rising to still grander organisms, we behold the wonderful and overpowering equilibrium which distinguishes the allied orbs which constitute the *cortège* of the sun. Here, again, I demand, has the sun, in and of itself, independent of God the Creator, the power to attract his dependent worlds? Have these orbs, as they roll and shine, the power, independent of God, to reciprocate this attractive power? Can the earth we inhabit put forth an energy independent of God, and bid the moon sway to its commanding and controlling power? This living force, this potent influence, is even denied to man, who thinks, and reasons, who lives, and hopes, and yet shall we attribute it to inert matter, dead, insensate, without one germ of living force?

True philosophy, I think, compels us to acknowledge that all the operations of nature, from the sweep of the planet down to the gentle sway of the bending floweret, are of and from the will of the Supreme momentarily exerted and put forth forever according to invariable laws.

We may propound, then, with propriety, how it comes to pass that the will of God momentarily exerted to sustain and carry forward the infinitely diversified and multitudinous operations of nature, should be exerted according to invariable laws? Here we stand on the threshold of a mighty inquiry, one that I can not here attempt to penetrate. But we can stand on the very threshold and affirm, that in case God did not govern himself in the exertion of His will in the physical universe by invariable laws, man could never rise to any correct knowledge of any thing external to himself. All human inquiry into nature is based on the grand assumption that nature's laws are absolutely invariable, and building on this corner-stone our solid substratum of inquiry, we ascend slowly but surely, from step to step, onward and upward, until the grand mysteries of nature stand revealed, and the glory and wisdom of God as displayed in the physical universe stand revealed.

If, then, the physical heavens and earth,—if the diverse organisms which fill the universe, were intended to educate the intellect, the soul, and the heart of man, unalterable laws, fixed as the being of God, lie at the foundation of the success of this grand design. No deviation or deviations from these laws can be admitted, unless in our weak judgment man's education may thereby be more rapidly and successfully accomplished.

The revelation of the Creator to the creature by any means short of those we denominate miraculous, except in so far as God declares

Himself in the laws of nature, is a matter sufficiently difficult, and perhaps even incomprehensible to man.

Let us for a moment admit that God has established the laws of nature, and that it is impossible for Him to suspend, modify, or abrogate any one of these laws, in what way can He possibly demonstrate to rational creatures the truth of any message He may desire to communicate? I remember once to have received a visit from a person of grave demeanor, wearing a long beard, long hair, a leathern girdle, a strange costume, and bearing a staff which he called Beauty, and proclaiming himself the prophet Elijah, sent direct from God to demand possession of the grounds I then occupied, to build thereon the city of the new Jerusalem. I at once demanded the credentials of this strange being. Let us admit him truly to have been sent from God, how upon the instant could he have demonstrated the truth of his claim in case the working of a miracle be impossible? If, however, on my demand he had lifted his hand to the sun, and at his command this mighty orb could have stood still in midst of heaven, or the lengthening shadow on the dial could have been turned back at his bidding, then I would have been compelled to acknowledge the command as coming from the Supreme, as the evidence would have been absolute and irresistible.

I contend, therefore, that miracles can not be excluded from the government of the Creator; that they form a medium of intercommunication with His creatures; that they must be employed whenever the education and moral elevation of humanity can be more perfectly or more rapidly accomplished by their use than by the uniform action of natural laws; and that it would be unphilosophical to reject altogether the evidence offered to prove the occurrence of a miraculous event.

With these general views we proceed to an examination of the miracles already alluded to as supposed to have been wrought, and the record of which is thought to be found in the Hebrew scriptures.

Let us admit the facts as generally received, that at the command of Joshua the sun and moon did stand still, and hastened not to go down for a whole day; and that there was no day like that before it or after it that the Lord hearkened to the voice of a man.

What special interference with the laws of motion and gravitation would be required to accomplish the results here demanded? To arrest the apparent motion of the sun and moon, it is only necessary to suspend the rotation of the earth on its axis. Its revolution in its orbit might continue uninterrupted; the moon's revolution around the earth, in like manner, might remain unaffected; and, indeed, the whole planetary system could not in the smallest degree be affected by any change in the period of rotation of the earth on its axis. But any sudden check in the velocity of rotation of the earth on its axis, would have a tendency to throw from its surface, especially near the equator. No sudden check, however, is required; and, indeed, a gradual diminution of the velocity of rotation might be made, such that in forty seconds the motion might cease entirely, and the change would not be sensible to the inhabitants of the earth except from the appearance of the heavens. It may then be asked, Did the miracle only require the gradual destruction of the rotation of the earth on its axis, and the restoration of the same? I answer that much more was demanded. The figure of the earth is such that the ocean, so far as it covers the equatorial regions, is sustained to a much higher level by the centrifugal force due to the velocity of rotation than would be compatible with its equilibrium in case this element of stability were destroyed. So that the direct interposition of the power of God would be required to not only suspend the earth's rotation, but also to prevent the equatorial oceans from rushing to the poles, and in their passage submerging the whole earth.

Such, then, are the physical demands in case the phenomenon of the standing still of the sun and moon were effected by arresting the rotation of the earth on its axis. While it does not involve a general suspension of the laws of gravitation and motion in the planetary system, it does demand the intervention of omnipotent power and the positive suspension of the laws of motion and gravitation in respect to the ocean which lies upon the earth's surface.

Is it then credible that the Supreme would thus interpose and exert His power to bring about the phenomenon described under the circumstances recorded? Here, as already urged, we can not reach any just conclusion. We can not know, except by revelation, why God may have found it necessary thus to interpose. His eye alone can pierce the dark curtain of the future, and His omniscience is alone capable of tracing such an event in its remote consequences, through the endless ages which are ever rolling on in the development of the great drama of creation.

If, then, the question be propounded, Can you credit a miracle involving the cessation of the rotation of the earth,—the equilibrium of the ocean during this cessation, and the restoration of the velocity of rotation,—I answer unequivocally Yes. If, however, the question be put, Do you give credence to evidence presented in the tenth chapter of the Book of

Joshua, regarded by some as proof of the miracle in question, I shall be compelled to answer, No.

To explain my meaning let me say again that He who built the heavens and established the laws of universal matter, who reveals Himself to His intelligent, moral, responsible creatures in the grandeur of the physical universe, can undoubtedly suspend, modify, or abrogate any one or all of His established laws; that He would never cut Himself off from the use of miraculous events in His moral government; and, lastly, that no law of nature would ever be suspended while the same result could be reached by the miraculous use of the established laws of nature. Admitting, still, that at Joshua's bidding the sun and moon stayed their course, and hastened not to go down even for the space of a whole day, there is another way in which this miraculous event could have been produced without in any degree interrupting the earth's rotation or suspending the laws of equilibrium which govern the heaving waters of the great deep.

It is well known that the atmosphere, in common with many transparent substances, possesses the power of refracting light so as to bend the rays from their rectilineal path, causing them to reach the eye even after the object whence they are emitted or reflected is already below the horizon. Thus we know that the sun, moon, and stars from this cause always remain visible for a short time after their setting below the horizon; and in fixing the place of a celestial body, astronomers are compelled to determine the laws of atmospheric refraction, and to apply to the apparent place a correction due to refraction to obtain the true place.

Here, then, we find among the laws of nature the means whereby the sun and moon, by miraculous power, might be made to remain permanently for hours in the same apparent place. By interposing a refracting medium of such variable density that the refractive power would precisely counteract the effect of the earth's rotation, the sun and moon might be made to stand still even for the space of a whole day. This would, indeed, be quite as miraculous as to arrest the earth's rotation, and would demand nothing less than the interposition of the divine omnipotence. No natural laws, operating within their usual limits, could produce any such effect; and while in this case we would be compelled to admit the miraculous character of the phenomenon, it is wrought by the aid of natural laws, and not in opposition to them.

Indeed, the miraculous retroversion of the shadow on the sun-dial of Ahaz, may readily be accounted for by supposing a miraculous interposition of a refracting medium sufficient to turn the sun apparently backward ten degrees in his diurnal circuit. Still the event is miraculous, and not according to the order of nature, but wrought out, as has been said, by the aid of natural laws.

While, then, we are willing to admit on credible testimony, even the suspension of the laws of motion and gravitation, that God may thereby the better administer the affairs of His moral government; and while we more readily admit the miraculous use of natural laws, we now come to consider whether it is unequivocally recorded in the Hebrew scriptures that the sun and moon stayed in their course at the command of Joshua, and "hasted not to go down for about the space of a whole day." And if such record is found to exist beyond reasonable doubt, does astronomical science now possess a sufficient knowledge of the movements of the sun and moon as to pronounce with certainty as to what were their relative positions on the date of the occurrence of the recorded event?

I do not profess any knowledge of the Hebrew, neither do I pretend to have made a profound examination of the passage in the tenth chapter of Joshua, in which this event is presumed to be recorded. It is sufficient for my purpose to state that able critics among the students of sacred literature have reached the conclusion that the declaration in question is a poetical quotation from the Book of Jasher, and hence the statement, "is not this written in the book of Jasher," or "the upright." This same book is quoted nearly in the same language in one of the other books of the Old Testament. So long, then, as there is any reasonable doubt as to the verity of the record, it would seem quite unnecessary to hold those who receive the Bible as a book of divine authority responsible for a miracle which seems to involve nothing less than the suspension of the laws of nature in that vast realm wherein uniformity seems to be most positively demanded.

Again, if we examine the record we find, that in case certain portions are omitted, in which this poetical quotation is involved, that the historical account is made more consistent with itself. We are told that Joshua came up to the aid of Gibeon, from Gilgal, by a forced march which continued all night. The battle with the five kings occurred the next day, in which they were discomfited, and fled before the army of Joshua, being pursued and destroyed by tempest and by hail-stones, "and there were more which died with the hail-stones, than they whom the children of Israel slew with the sword." If now we omit verses 12, 13, 14, 15, and 16, the narrative continues: "And it was told Joshua, saying, The five kings are found in a cave at Makkedah." But if these verses be retained, we are told, in the fifteenth verse, that Joshua returned to Gilgal and all Israel with him, and no mention whatever is made of his coming again to Makkedah, to complete the conquest of this and the other four cities which were destroyed, after the conquest of which it is again said that Joshua and all Israel with him returned to the camp at Gilgal, precisely as in the fifteenth verse.

There seems, therefore, a reasonable doubt as to the correctness of the record, and as to whether this seeming record of miraculous interposition, by the arrest of the apparent motion of the sun and moon, may not be a mere quotation from some ancient Hebrew poem now lost.

Indeed the defeat and destruction of the Amorites seems to have been complete. They fled before Israel and were destroyed by the hail-storm from Beth-horon to Azekah, and after this signal destruction and already miraculous victory, we are told that Joshua spake unto the Lord, and he said in the sight of all Israel, "Sun, stand thou still on Gibeon, and thou moon in the valley of Ajalon." This prolonging of the day does not seem to be necessary under the circumstances, and so soon as our suspicion is aroused as to the genuineness of the passage, we see many reasons to confirm this suspicion. But we will leave this, where it properly belongs, to biblical critics, and return to the consideration of the question, Does our present knowledge of the relative motions of the sun and moon enable us to decide whether any such miracle has been absolutely performed?

To bring this question within the legitimate scope of astronomical investigation, we must admit that the miracle was performed, not by the interposition of a refracting medium, which made the sun and moon appear to stand still, but by a positive cessation of the motion of rotation of the earth on its axis, whereby a day was increased in length by a certain number of hours, amounting to, say, from eight to twelve.

The event under consideration took place about one thousand four hundred years B. C., and consequently more than three thousand two hundred years ago. Can the science of Astronomy go back to so remote a period, and pronounce with certainty as to the relative positions of the sun and moon? In case it be possible to determine the relative positions of Gibeon and Ajalon, such is our present knowledge of the apparent motions of the sun and moon, that we could compute backward and pronounce with certainty, that on a given day, in a given year, the sun and moon either did or did not hold the places assigned them.

The most complex, profound, and involved problem ever presented for human investigation is this very one to predict, or compute, the relative places of the sun and moon, as seen by a spectator on the earth's surface. It involves every delicacy of instrumental observation, the entire depth and power of mathematical analysis, every artifice of computation, and a full knowledge of the numerous orbs which constitute the mighty system which owes allegiance to the sun. And yet, we have reason to believe that after a struggle of six thousand years, involving the best talent, the most powerful genius, the most elaborate effort, the problem is finally solved, and almost at the very time we write. It is possible to unwind the tangled and confused pathway of the moon among the stars, and to unroll the golden thread spun by the solar orb, in the long centuries of its past revolutions, and to pronounce with certainty, that on a given day, at a given hour, the sun did or did not stand over Gibeon, while the moon did or did not stand over the valley of Ajalon.

This is now demonstrated by the computation and ancient eclipses of the sun and moon, eclipses observed and recorded more than two thousand years ago. Whenever, then, the exact geographical position of Joshua's camp shall have been determined,—when we shall learn where is Gibeon and the valley of Ajalon,—when we shall come to know at what season of the year this great battle was fought, in what month and on what day of the month the Hebrew warrior won his great victory,—then we can pronounce with positive certainty that the place assigned to the sun over Gibeon and that given to the moon over Ajalon were or were not those occupied by these celestial orbs on the date of this miraculous event. If, indeed, the earth's rotation were then suspended,—if, at the bidding of

God, its swift revolution on its "noiseless axle" slowly died away,—if by miraculous power the equilibrium of the ocean were maintained, and its stupendous wave was upheld by the hand of Divine Omnipotence,—these extraordinary events must stand out full, positive, absolute. For here there will be a break, a gap, a hiatus created by this cessation of the earth's rotation for the space of a whole day, in uniform recurrence of day and night; and the astronomical phenomena prior to this wonderful day and those subsequent to it can only be reconciled on the supposition that the day was prolonged to double its usual length.

But let us admit that astronomical science and computation have the power to trace back the sun and moon, and pronounce their relative positions five thousand years ago; let us admit that eclipses recorded before the time of Joshua, when compared with those recorded since his time, demonstrate the uniform and uninterrupted rotation of the earth on its axis; let us admit that the most satisfactory and indubitable evidence of the geographical positions of Gibeon and Ajalon are reached, and the date of Joshua's victory is fixed beyond doubt or cavil; and that astronomical computation shows that while the sun rested over Gibeon, the moon did hang over the valley of Ajalon,—what will all this show? Simply and solely that the miraculous arrest of the sun and moon was not accomplished by the stoppage of the earth's rotation. But in case astronomy, pointed to the above facts, demonstrates that while the sun actually rested over Gibeon the moon could not have hung over Ajalon, then we shall be compelled to conclude that the event has been interpolated from some ancient Hebrew poem now forever lost.

The second miracle of power,—the retreat of the shadow on the sun-dial of Ahaz,—has been already sufficiently considered, and may be so obviously produced by the interposition of a refracting medium, that any further notice seems quite superfluous.

From the preceding discussion the question may arise, How can we be assured that God ever does positively interrupt any of the laws of nature? In the miracle just considered, how could we become assured that the sun and moon were positively arrested by the cessation of the earth's rotation? In short, should a professed messenger from God at this day stand upon the earth and command the sun and moon to stay their course in mid-heaven, how can we pronounce this to be the effect of a refracting medium, or the result of the actual stoppage of the earth's axial revolution?

Our present knowledge of the physical structure of the universe is such that we could not mistake for one moment the real nature of the miracle. Should the rotation of the earth on its axis be increased by five seconds of time in twenty-four hours, all the time-keepers in all the watch-towers of the world would proclaim the fact,—all the stars would fail to keep their appointed meridian transits, and would, in sympathy with the great orbs of light, linger in their nocturnal march. The bursting out in the heavens of a thousand fiery comets in a single night could produce no such mortal terror to the astronomer as this falling backward of the mighty sphere of the starry universe for one single second in twenty-four hours, for it would speak the doom of the universe in announcing that God's right arm was growing heavy, and His omnipotent will was commencing to stagger under the weight of ten millions of rolling worlds. Should such an event ever occur,—should the time ever come when indeed those shining sentinels in the high heavens should fail to keep their appointed vigils,—when the astronomer shall look wistfully through "optic tube" for the coming of the faithful star which, prompt to the thousandth of a single second, has traversed his meridian line, and, lo! the star lingers in its journey, seconds ebb slowly away and merge into minutes, and at last the star appears, no matter if with its wonted beauty, the astronomer stands aghast, and well may he tremble, for the powers of the heavens are smitten, and God is deserting the universe which sprang into being at His divine command. Human confidence and faith would be gone forever, and no remedy could avail to rectify the wrong.

We have no fears that our confidence will ever be thus rudely shaken, not because we believe nature and her laws to be eternal, not because we believe that this stupendous mechanism has endured from all eternity,—for even then after countless revolutions, a fault, an anomaly, a failure in the series of sequences might occur, and, with its terrific utterance, announce the possible running down or destruction of the mechanism, but because I believe that God the Eternal, All-wise, Incomprehensible, created and now sustains all things by the word of His power: it is because of God's eternity that we dwell in simple trust upon an unshaken order, and a purpose to be achieved.

Before closing this subject, it may be expected that something shall be said of those remarkable passages in the New Testament, in which are set forth in prophetic language, at once sublime and terrific, the final doom of the earth we inhabit. Is it credible that this earth is to be consumed by fire,—that the sun and moon are to be darkened,—that the stars of heaven are to fall,—that the skies are to be wrapped in flame, and to be rolled up as a scroll,—are these oriental figures or dread realities, which at no distant day are to strike terror to the inhabitants of earth?

I frankly confess I do not know how to answer these questions, and I do not believe that all the science and philosophy which now exists on earth, can fit an individual one particle for their comprehension or solution. There are those who find in the internal structure of the earth,—its volcanoes with their rivers of molten lava,—evidences that these sublime predictions are one day to be accomplished. I dare not thus point out to the All-wise the means to accomplish his purposes. I can only bow and reverently accept. And do you really believe that the day will ever come, when this great globe, with its rock-ribbed mountains, shall melt with fervent heat,—its ocean billows flash into unmeasured volumes of fiery steam, — when flaming fire shall wrap the doomed planet and devour its very being, and blot it from its kindred family of worlds? I can only answer that I know of no special reason why this earth should be eternal. Its destruction does not involve the well-being of the universe, and were it even blotted from existence it would but momentarily disturb the equilibrium of the great scheme of worlds, of which it forms an insignificant unit. But should God destroy its present form; should it indeed be baptized with fire; should it be purged and purified, God can bring it out of this terrific ordeal, not one atom of His matter lost, but all remodeled, restored, recreated, a new world filled with beauty, and joy, and perpetual happiness; where death—the wages of sin—shall never appear, and where neither tears, nor sobs, nor sorrows shall dim the beauty of its enchanting abodes.

Of all these things I am profoundly ignorant; but the moment the mind grasps the great idea of an ever-living, ever-active, ever-present God, the Creator and Supporter of all things, our Father and our Friend, then all subordinate difficulties vanish. There we cast the anchor of our faith, sure and steadfast, and no doubt can ever arise, to fling its darkness and gloom over the unruffled sea on which we calmly float.

To this point have my investigations, and studies, and thoughts, and observations in the heavens and in the earth, in physical nature and in human thought, in matter and in mind, brought me with irresistible power. As a physical philosopher, I am compelled to believe in God; as a believer in God, I am compelled to accept the great truth, that He can reveal himself by miraculous power. As a student of the economy, and order, and perpetuity of God's government, I am compelled to believe that no miracle will be wrought by the suspension or temporary abrogation of the laws of nature, which are God's uniform expressions of His Divine will, when the same may be accomplished by the miraculous use of natural laws. As a thinking, sentient, loving, suffering, willing, being, I am compelled to lift myself, and all my race, immeasurably above the myriad worlds that roll and shine in space, and declare that a single tear ebbing from the heart of humble sorrow, is of more value, in the sight of God, than a legion of suns. The moral, then, towers infinitely above the material, and it is only to give to the moral greater strength, and beauty, and grandeur, that God has organized the material, and whenever in the rolling ages Divine wisdom shall decide that one atom can be added to the moral by the total subversion of the material, then the sun and moon shall be darkened, the stars shall fall, the elements shall melt with fervent heat, the heavens shall be rolled up as a scroll, and, out of this seeming destruction, a new heaven and a new earth shall appear radiant with beauty, and eternally crowned with the blessings of God, and with never-ending light and glory.

LECTURE VII.

THE LANGUAGE OF THE BIBLE.

LECTURE VII.

THE LANGUAGE OF THE BIBLE.

It is our purpose now to consider the current language employed by the writers of the sacred volume in speaking of the physical universe. There never has been a time, when those ignorant of any science, could employ that science and its facts intelligently in any composition, for the very language used would inevitably reveal the fact, that the writer could have no just idea of the science to which he ventured to make reference. This remark must remain true, when applied to the writers of the various books of the Bible. It is in vain to say that the grandeur of the nocturnal heavens, the glittering splendors of the starry sphere, the dazzling glory of the sun, and the milder effulgence of the moon and planets, must have inspired exalted ideas in all ages. This is quite as true of all the ancient historical nations, as of the Hebrews. The Babylonians, the Assyrians, the Persians, Greeks, and Romans, beheld the same heavens and were illuminated by the same splendors which shone on the Hebrew prophets and the Hebrew poets, and yet none of these ancient nations reached any such exalted conceptions, or recorded in language so just and so sublime, the direct dependence of the created universe on God the omnipotent Creator.

Thus we find in the oldest book of the Hebrew scriptures, in the very first sentence of that most mysterious of volumes, the simple sublime declaration, *In the beginning God created the heavens and the earth.* There is no argument,—no train of complex reasoning on the relations of the material and immaterial,—no profound research into the origin of matter, its qualities and properties, its creation and primordial condition or its eternal existence,—there is no talk of a former chaos, and old night, and the omnipotent energy put forth to quell the chaotic confusion and to educe harmony and beauty;—not one word of all this, but simply and sublimely, "*In* the beginning God created the heavens and the earth."

When we compare this language and declaration with the origin of all things as given by the most ancient nations, we can not fail to be struck with its vast superiority. The Egyptian priests, according to Herodotus, ascribe all things to a great winged egg; the Persians, if we are to credit Eusebius, made the principle of the universe a gloomy and tempestuous atmosphere. From this gloomy and tempestuous atmosphere first sprang a wind; this wind, becoming enamored of its own principle, produced desire or love, and from this love, with the wind as father, first came mind, and hence all the generations of the universe.

If it be asserted that these are but the wild dreams of barbarians, let us examine for a moment the theories of the refined and philosophic Greeks. Thales, the Ionian, and the founder of a philosophic sect, made water the universal principle; Plato, the prince of Greek philosophers, maintained that the universe was simply arranged by the power of God, but that the

Deity was incapable of such a creation; Aristotle adopted the philosophy of Plato; Zeno maintained that the universe, as it now exists, was brought into order by its own energy; while Epicurus asserted that all things had sprung from a fortuitous concourse of atoms.

He who now scans the magnificence and grandeur of the celestial mechanism,—who surveys the sublime equilibrium of the rolling worlds which circle round the sun, swaying and swayed, disturbing and disturbed, ever changing and never changed, rolling on from eternity to eternity,—will be compelled to adopt the language of the Hebrew leader and lawgiver, "In the beginning God created the heavens and the earth." If we extend our researches beyond the limit of the sun's domain, sweeping beyond the orbit of the farthest planet, and ever leaving behind us the utmost verge of the comets' sweep, penetrating the region of the blazing stars, and traveling in the might of human thought and human vision, from universe to universe, here surrounded by systems of mysterious organization, with an equilibrium of motion as sublime and solid as eternity,—we instinctively adopt the language of Moses the servant of God, and exclaim, *In the beginning God created the heavens and the earth.*

The same sublime simplicity pervades the entire account given by Moses, of the order of creation. The Spirit of God moved on the face of the waters; and God said, Let there be light, and there was light. And God said, Let the earth bring forth. And God made man in His own image, and breathed into his nostrils the breath of life, and he became a living creature. And these are the generations of the heavens and the earth, in the day that the Lord God created the heavens and the earth.

The problem presented for solution is simply this: Does an intimate knowledge of the universe as developed by the grand discoveries of modern science, cause these declarations to sink into insignificance, or to rise to grander and more stupendous proportions? It can not be denied that such a knowledge as we now possess of the structure of the heavens, does cause the doctrine of the Egyptians, Persians, and Greeks, as already sketched, to appear simply ridiculous. I use the only words which can express my meaning. Even the philosophy of Plato which elevates matter above God, and asserts the power of the Omnipotent to extend only to the organization and not to creation, can not satisfy the demands of the mind imbued with a full knowledge of the revelations of modern science. We are compelled to go backward to the beginning, and propound the mighty interrogatory, Whence sprang the matter of which these multitudinous worlds were formed? Whence the mysterious and incomprehensible principle of light? Whence the still more mysterious and incomprehensible principle of vegetable life? And whence the breath of life, whereby man became a living soul, with thought and reason, joy, sorrow, and love? These questions must be answered, and we find the only satisfactory response in the language of the Bible: God hath created all things and sustaineth all things, by the word of His power.

Leaving this great topic of creation, which we shall treat hereafter more at large, and which we now only mention for the purpose of noting the language employed by the Hebrew writer, let us pass to an examination of the doctrine of God's providence, as displayed in the maintenance of absolute rule in the physical universe.

There are, doubtless, philosophers and astronomers, who in their mathematical and astronomical investigations, leave out of the great problem of nature the very being of God. This, indeed, in the very nature of things they are compelled to do. No power of analytical grasp, no refinement of infinitesimal arithmetic can reach the being and attributes of God. The philosopher and mathematician is compelled to begin exactly where Moses left off. In the beginning God created the heavens and the earth, says Moses, and admitting this declaration, the philosopher undertakes to discover the plan according to which this creation was effected, and by means of which it is now maintained. The sun, the moon, the planets, the comets, the stars, exist; they roll and shine, measuring time by their mighty revolutions, and filling space by their sublime orbits. There they are as God created them, and the philosopher simply inquires, According to what laws do they move? What reciprocal influences do they exert? What are the forms and limits of their mighty orbits? What the sublime periods of their march through space? What the nature of the dynamic equilibrium which links them into groupings of surpassing grandeur?

It is true that in all these investigations the very being of God may be forgotten. For the lawgiver we may substitute the laws. Gravitation may supersede, in mathematical research, the omnipotence of God. The laws of motion, simple, invariable, eternal, may stand for that attribute of Jehovah's will which changeth not, the same, yesterday, to-day and forever. The sun himself may be shorn of his effulgence: his light, and heat, and life, may shrink and fade beneath the withering breath of philosophy, and this mighty and glorious orb become a material heavy point, and all the revolving planets and their moons, other material heavy points, at definite distances, and with determinate weights, and thus the will of God, as manifested in His laws, and the very creations of God as exhibited in his suns, and systems, and moving worlds, become the mere hypotheses and material points in the diagram of the mathematician's slate,—and what then? Does this destroy God and his attributes? Does this blot out of the heavens the blazing sun? Does this strike from being, planet, and moon, and earth teeming with life, and hope, and joy, and love, and immortality?— Never! They all remain: while the geometer grapples these wondrous orbs in their weight, dimensions, distances, and motions, with his sublime analytic machinery, and with gigantic intellectual power follows their grand career,— the problem solved, the orbit figured, the period predicted,—all, all proclaim the being of God, the unchangeableness of the laws of His physical government, and the grasp of thought with which He has endowed His own image, into whose nostrils He breathed the breath of life.

It has been truly sung:

"The undevout astronomer is mad——"

and yet, alas! we are compelled in a few instances to confess, that this madness has filled the hearts of some whose names have been written in letters of living light, on the very circle of the heavens. I say a few instances, for by far the greater number of the heroes of science are to be counted among the devout. Copernicus, and Kepler, and Tycho, and Galileo, and the prince of philosophers, Newton the immortal—all looked through nature to nature's God's. Kepler, in all his grand investigations, commenced his daily toil by invoking the aid of Divine wisdom, and Newton's reverence was so great, that he never uttered the name of God without reverently lifting his hand to his head, feeling the immediate presence of the divinity in His material works. And, yet, these are the greatest names which the annals of astronomy and science can boast,—their investigations were more profound, their mathematics deeper than most of those could boast, who are now compelled to acknowledge themselves humble followers of these great luminaries. We say, then, that while in minds especially framed for pure *physical* research, there is a tendency to and undue preponderance of mathematical reasoning, the abstractions of science, and the mathematics of astronomy, do not of necessity lead to skepticism.

In the writers of the Hebrew Scriptures, there is no exhibition of a knowledge of physical science, no mathematical investigations. Simple declarations are made, and these declarations are either in coincidence with or opposed to what science now teaches, and it is the language employed in the declaration which we propose to re-examine.

In proclaiming the majesty of God, the Hebrew prophet exclaims: "Lift up your eyes on high, and behold! He hath created all these things that bringeth out their hosts by number, He calleth them all by names by the greatness of His might." Again, the same prophet proclaims, that "God hath measured the waters in the hollow of His hand, and meted out the heavens with a span, and comprehended the dust of the earth in a measure, and weighed the mountains in scales, and the hills in a balance." The Hebrew poet, addressing the Almighty, uses this sublime language: "O Lord my God, thou art very great; thou art clothed with honor and with majesty: who coverest thyself with light as with a garment: who stretchest out the heavens like a curtain: who maketh the clouds his chariot: who walketh on the wings of the wind: who laid the foundations of the earth, that it should not be removed forever. Thou coverest it with the deep as with a garment." So Job declares that God by His spirit hath garnished the heavens, His hand hath formed the crooked serpent: lo! these are a part of His ways, but the thunders of His power who can understand! Again, the same old author in that sublime chapter in which the Lord answers out of the whirlwind, asks: "Knowest thou the ordinances of heaven, and canst thou set the dominion thereof on the earth?"

It is needless to multiply quotations. Throughout the entire volumes of the Old and New Testament, there is is but one opinion expressed by every writer in every age, and that opinion not only ascribes to God the creation of all things, by the word of His power, but God is represented as momentarily sustaining the universe, upholding all things by His Divine command.

Are these views and expressions in accordance with the present knowledge of the physical universe? When we have gone from the sun, with its stupendous dimensions, through the planetary orbs; when we have examined their admirable organization, and their exquisite equilibrium; when we behold the paths they describe, and the ceaseless cycles they fulfil; when amidst never-ending changes we find the earth linked to its orbit with fetters of adamant; when we behold the admirable adjustment of sun, and planet, and satellite, so that in all the revolving ages, seed-time and harvest, summer and winter, and day and night, shall never fail; when with telescopic power we fathom the profundity of space, and visit the island universes that stretch away in a vast illimitable perspective; when suns and systems tower in grandeur on the right hand and on the left, and the womb of space teems with glittering worlds like sands on the seashore;—with thoughts thus expanded and touching the infinite; with the soul aglow with sublimity; with aspirations exalted, let us turn to the language of the Bible, and learn whether it exalts the sensations and sentiments we feel or crushes them by its weakness and impotency. Let the answer come from the Hebrew Psalmist, from the prophets, from the language of those grand apocalyptic visions of St. John. I care not where it be selected, it furnishes the only fitting vehicle to express the thoughts that overwhelm us; and we break out involuntarily in the language of God's own inspiration: "The heavens declare the glory of God, the firmament showeth his handywork. Day unto day uttereth speech, and night unto night showeth forth knowledge." "When I consider thy heavens the work of thy fingers, the moon and the stars which thou hast ordained; Lord, what is man, that thou art mindful of him, or the son of man that thou visitest him." "If I take the wings of the morning and fly to the uttermost parts of the earth, lo! thou art there; if I ascend to the heaven of heavens, lo! thy presence filleth immensity. Thou, and thou alone art God over all, and blessed forever!"

Let us examine some of these wonderful declarations with more critical attention, and learn whether they will bear the test of severe analysis. "The heavens declare the glory of God, and the firmament showeth forth His handy-work." The glory of an earthly monarch is derived from the extent and variety of his empire; from the perfection of his laws and perfect manner in which they are administered; and from the consequent happiness and prosperity of his subjects. God's empire as displayed in the material universe, is thus far immeasurable : no sounding line or telescopic ray has ever flung its plummet so deep, as to measure its vast profundity. The dimensions of the sun's domain are such as to defy the power of human conception adequately to grasp. Who can conceive the magnitude of the orbit of Neptune, revolving at a distance from the sun of no less than three thousand millions of miles? But this is only a minute atom, when we come to consider the distance of the fixed stars, whose average distance from the sun must exceed the distance of Neptune in the enormous ratio of twenty thousand to one;

so that while the light of Neptune may reach the sun in five hours, that from the fixed stars of greatest magnitude, will occupy not less than ten years.

This brings us to the nearest portion of that vast congeries of stars which we denominate the Milky Way, composed of not less than one hundred millions of suns, and of such vast proportions, that light flashing at the rate of twelve millions of miles in a single minute could not cross its deepest range in less than ten thousand years. Leaving the Milky Way and plunging yet deeper into space, we find other milky ways grander and more populous in stars even than our own, until at last our telescopic ray extends so deeply, that its length, furnishing a journey for the swift wing of light of more than three millions of years, fails to plunge across any other mighty depth, and we stand wondering and awestruck on the very threshold of infinitude.

These statements are not vague conjectures; they are founded in the clearest reasoning, and if there be any error it is rather in contracting than expanding the just limits of the visible universe. The heavens, then, in their vast, incomprehensible dimensions, and in the uncounted millions of their clustering orbs, proclaim the glory of God's empire.

If now we direct our attention to the laws by which this vast empire is governed, we find them absolutely perfect. Every atom that floats in the sunbeam; every planet that wheels through space; every sun with its family of worlds; every island universe; all obey the grand laws by which absolute perfection reigns wherever matter fills the womb of space. These laws are not only perfect, but they are perfectly administered. They change not. In all the ages past there comes up no evidence that gravitation and motion have ever for a single moment relaxed their power. But these laws in and of themselves are incapable of producing a system. They could not create the sun, or select the planets, or project their orbits. This demanded the wisdom and power of God. When we behold the delicate equilibrium which characterizes the sun's system, in which world is balanced against world, and satellite against satellite, in which not one of these multitudinous orbs could be displaced, without destroying the harmony and perfection of the whole,— in which each planet and satellite affects the movement of every other, to their disturbing powers a limit being fixed beyond which they can never pass, so that for countless millions of ages, the earth shall roll on in its orbit, giving to its inhabitants seed-time and harvest, and summer and winter, and, forever silently revolving on its well-poised axle, shall teach the dayspring from on high to keep its place, and day and night to preserve perpetual covenant with God,—we are again led to exclaim :—"Surely the heavens declare the glory of God, and the firmament showeth forth his handywork!"

These results are not the offspring of accident, they are not the evolutions of blind fatality, they are the arrangements of an ever-living omnipotent, omniscient power, who can be none other than God the Creator. Wisdom infinite, is written all over the universe. Wisdom was with God from all eternity, from everlasting, from the beginning, or ever the earth was. When there were no depths, wisdom was brought forth,—so hath the finger of inspiration written—" while as yet He had not made the earth nor the fields. When He prepared the heavens I was there : when He set a compass on the face of the depth : when He established the clouds above : when He strengthened the fountains of the deep: when He gave to the sea His decree, that the waters should not pass His commandment: when He appointed the foundations of the earth." The wisdom of God reigns supreme throughout the manifold works of His creation. Thus is it written in the word of God, and thus is it recorded in the celestial machinery which is recorded on high.

We are now so much accustomed to the employment of the language of the Bible, in the expression of our thoughts concerning nature, that we scarcely recognize the astonishing character of the fact that this harmony exists. We are almost led to the conclusion that it could not be otherwise, the language is so exact and so apposite ; the expressions so powerful, that it would seem that he who coined these phrases must have possessed an intimate knowledge of the objects to which they are applied.

We must constantly bear in mind the fact, that all the books of the Bible were closed before the dawn of modern science. No knowledge of the true mechanism of the universe then existed, and for ages after the last book of the Hebrew scriptures was written and the revelation sealed, a false system prevailed and exerted an unbroken sway over the human mind. Had this old doctrine of Ptolemy, the Greek astronomer, been demonstrated to be absolutely true, then the superlative language of the Bible could not have been applied, and the heavens would not have declared the glory of God, neither would the firmament have shown forth his handywork. The complexity and cumbrousness of the Ptolemaic system grew to such vast dimensions, that human genius revolted, and reached the conclusion :—either that such a universe had not sprung from the hand of an omniscient God, or that the true system of nature remained to be discovered.

Indeed at the time when Galileo attacked with

so much power the hoary doctrines of the Greek astronomers, and when the Church ignorantly fearing lest faith in the inspiration of the Bible might be shaken by the subversion of the Ptolemaic system, with what vehemence might Galileo have retorted, that these same sacred books assert that the heavens declare the glory of God, that the firmament showeth His handywork; that God had created all things in wisdom and by the word of His power; that it was only by abandoning these false systems that it became possible to verify the declarations of the sacred text; that as there was but one God, so there could be only one single plan throughout the created universe.

. Let us now pass from these general expressions of scripture, to those which are more specific. It may be contended that the language we have cited would naturally flow from a contemplation of the splendid spectacle presented in the nocturnal heavens, and that the power of an eastern imagination has been wonderfully successful in picturing the true glories of the universe.

We find in the Hebrew prophets an occasional use of astronomical facts, to affirm and intensify a declaration. Thus, when God would illustrate the perpetuity of His covenant with Israel, the prophet is made to employ no less than five astronomical illustrations to affirm this truth with greater power and cogency. "Thus saith the Lord, who giveth the sun for a light by day, and the ordinances of the moon, and the stars, for a light by night, if these ordinances depart from before me then may my promise fail." "If heaven above can be measured, and the foundations of the earth searched out from beneath, then and not till then will I cast off my people." "If ye can break my covenant of the day, and my covenant of the night, and that there should not be day and night in their season; then may my covenant be broken with my servant David." "As the host of heaven can not be numbered, so will I multiply the seed of David." "If my covenant be not with day and night, and if I have not appointed the ordinances of heaven and earth, then will I cast away the seed of Jacob."

Here, then, are five distinct declarations:

That God had appointed the ordinances of heaven and earth; the laws by which all the material worlds are governed and that these laws could never change.

That He had made a covenant with day and night, absolutely irreversible, so that so long as time should last there should be day and night in their season.

That the host of heaven could not be numbered.

That the foundations of the earth could not be searched out from beneath; and, that the heavens above could never be measured or their mighty depths sounded, by any power of man's device.

Let us proceed to examine these topics in order. The ordinances of Heaven and earth,— the laws of the physical universe, are never severed,—so in Job : " Knowest thou the ordinances of heaven, and canst thou set the dominion thereof on the earth." Thus, these laws whatever they may be, exert their dominion over the objects that shine in the heavens as well as upon the earth we inhabit. It is, surely, a remarkable fact that the heavens and the earth are thus inseparably united, in the language of the Hebrew scriptures, when they are invariably treated with positive severance by all the writers of all the primitive nations of which we have any record. And yet this grand truth has but just been revealed by modern science. The law of universal gravitation and the laws of motion, sweep under their dominion the sun, and moon, and planets, and comets, even the distant stars, and to this grand list we now add the earth itself, in its mass, and in every particle which constitutes its mass. Every drop of its ocean; every atom of its cloudy vapors; every particle of its rugged mountains, and broad-spread continents; even the very invariable atmosphere, which like a garment of beauty wraps the earth, is subject to these same laws. This absolute unity, this oneness of matter, is one of the most overwhelming facts of modern science, and yet the ordinances of the gleaming heavens and the solid earth are one and indivisible. But do the conditions of these laws of matter and their perpetuity present a fit emblem to illustrate the inviolable nature of a promise made by Him who changeth not, who is the Father of light, in whom there is no variableness (parallax), nor shadow of change? I answer, that there is no way by which we can fitly illustrate the perpetuity of God's covenant, but by this very invariableness of the ordinances of heaven and earth. From age to age throughout the countless millions of years which have poured into the ocean of the past, and throughout the innumerable millions which constitute an eternity to come, we have reason to believe these laws will never change. He who framed them enacted them in wisdom. He sent forth His decree, and it stood fast. He commanded, and they were created: He hath established them for ever and ever!

We have already examined the nature of the covenant with day and night, and have marked the admirable exactitude of the earth's rotation on its axis. Could any more forcible illustration be given of the unchangeable nature of a promise made by Him who taught the dayspring from on high to know its place.

"The host of heaven can not be numbered."

In case the stars visible to the unaided vision of man had constituted the entire universe, this would have been a very feeble illustration of the multitudes which should be found among the posterity of Israel. The stars visible to the naked eye have all been numbered and their places fixed, so that not one can disappear without its loss shall become at once manifest. The actual number of stars visible to the eye of man does not exceed six or seven thousand, though in looking upon a clear sky, on a starlight night, the number seems to be vastly greater. At the time this passage was written, the host of heaven could not have been numbered, and the very instrument which rendered the numbering of the then visible host possible brought under the gaze of man hundreds of thousands of stars which had never before been seen. Every accession of telescopic power; every advance of human skill and human genius, but the more clearly demonstrates the utter impossibility of numbering the hosts of heaven. The innumerable stars that powder the zone of the Milky Way to the naked eye, find even in the most powerful telescopes their exact counterpart in other universes so deeply sunk in space, that the individual suns which compose their vast dimensions are seen but as a faint gleam of luminous haze even when we approach, transported by telescopic power, to within the thousandth part of their actual distance.

If the hosts of heaven can not be numbered, so, also, it is impossible to measure the heavens. We have, indeed, reached to a tolerable knowledge of the planetary distances,—and even the flight of the comet has been approximately measured; but thus far the stars have nearly defied the utmost stretch of human skill and science. A few years since, Bessel, the great German astronomer, announced that he had measured the distance of a double star in the Constellation of the Swan. It was a work to crown its author with immortality. Subsequent investigations have confirmed measurably the results of Bessel; but to show the exceeding difficulty of the problem, I need only remark that the Russian astronomer, Otto Struve, has recently published an elaborate discussion of this great subject, and has reached conclusions which differ from those of Bessel by a third part of the values reached by the latter; so that a parallactic angle fixed by Bessel at thirty-six hundreds of one second of arc is determined by Struve to be fifty hundredths of the same unit. The discrepancy between these results can only be made manifest by considering the actual difference in the distance of two stars whose parallaxes are represented by thirty-six and by fifty hundredths of one second of arc. Light would reach us from a star whose parallax is thirty-six hundredths of one second of arc in about ten years; while the light from a star with a parallax of fifty hundreds of a second would reach us in about six years. Thus the discrepancy amounts to a distance such that light flying at the rate of twelve millions of miles in every minute, would not pass it in less than four years! And yet this star is the one whose distance has been most perfectly measured. What shall we say, then, of the possibility of measuring the depth of those vast promontories of stars which distinguish the Milky Way, where star is ranged behind star until the stratum is five hundred deep! or who can conceive of the power of those instruments which shall define the distances of the clusters and nebulæ that stretch out to infinitude, and proclaim that the heavens can never be measured?

I have already considered the meaning of the expression, "the foundations of the earth," and have shown from the passage in Job that the writers seemed to comprehend that these foundations could never be discovered, for God, who stretched out the north over the empty place, "founded the earth upon nothing." And yet the earth is "established forever;" that is, the condition in which it now exists, the figure of its orbit, the mean annual temperature, the seasons, the recurrence of day and night, all that goes to render the earth habitable, shall continue forever. This seems to be the declaration of the sacred volume; and if science has read aright the structure of the planetary worlds, these facts are in an equal manner taught by the discoveries of modern science.

Thus we find an aptness and propriety in all

these astronomical illustrations employed by the Hebrew prophet, which are not weakened in their power, but amazingly strengthened when viewed in the full light of our present knowledge of the natural universe.

If there be those who still insist that this is all accidental, and that it would have been quite impossible to have blundered in drawing illustrations from the unchanging revolutions of Nature, I answer that nothing would have been easier than to have erred in this very direction. Suppose the prophet had pointed the Hebrews to the polar star, the object that had for centuries guided their ancestors in their wanderings and journeys, and had uttered the exclamation, "Behold yonder star, fixed immovable while all else is in motion; when that star shall swing away from its fixed position, then may the purpose of God fail toward the people of His choice." Now, nothing could have been more appropriate or seemingly more natural than the use of such a similitude, and yet at this day it would have been false, for the North Star has been slowly departing from its fixed position;

and, should the earth continue, the time will come when it will be compelled to yield its place, which another star will assume in its turn, to be displaced as the revolving ages roll on.

Thus we find a remarkable appropriateness in the selections which have been made of the phenomena of the heavens, to illustrate the teachings of prophetic declaration. They were appropriate to the age in which they were written, they have been appropriate in all succeeding ages down to the present time, and science assures us they can now never fail. Can all this have resulted from accident? Can so great a multitude of thoughts, expressions, doctrines, illustrations, and similitudes, have all risen by accident into appropriate use among so many writers, so widely separated in time? If it be argued that after all there is nothing in all this language, in all these expressions, in all these illustrations, and that it is but the perversions of an ingenious fancy which gives to them an appearance of appropriateness, it must still be admitted that it is certainly very wonderful that such a multitude of independent expressions should be capable of being woven into a texture of astonishing harmony and beauty.

I will not further multiply examples. Search the old prophets, the Psalms, the book of Job, even the New Testament, and in all these books, wherever any allusion is made to the physical heavens, it seems to have been written by one possessing the highest intelligence, the most profound knowledge.

There is but one solitary instance in which an author of any one book in the Bible, was brought face to face with the philosophy of antiquity. This was the celebrated meeting between the great Apostle of the Gentiles with the Stoics and Epicureans, on Mars' Hill, in Athens. As already stated, the Stoics did not admit the power of God to create the material of the universe. He could only arrange and organize what had existed from all eternity. He could banish old Night and subdue the empire of Chaos, but had no creative power. The Epicureans on the other hand were atheists, or at least their theism severed the divinity from all concern in either the physical or moral universe. As the existent condition of matter, its organization into suns and systems, and vegetable and animal life, were all the result of accident, of course the philosophers of this school did not admit the providence of God.

Paul, who was learned in the Hebrew scriptures, and who had been educated in the law at the feet of Gamaliel, even as a Jew, and much more as a Christian, had imbibed the doctrine so universally taught in the Bible, that all nature is but the offspring of the creative energy of the Divine will.

Here we find, then, the representatives of the doctrines of the Old and New Testament, both in philosophy and religion—the two great concerns of humanity—brought face to face with the philosophers and priests of Paganism, and under circumstances of most extraordinary grandeur.

The scene was the Areopagus, on Mars Hill, the most venerated and revered court of all antiquity. Here, in seats hewn from the solid rocks, sat the judges, whose decree fixed not only the fate of individuals, but of empires. On every hand the temples of the Pagan divinities reared their beautiful or majestic forms. Statues of men, heroes, and gods, in uncounted numbers, filled every niche and crowned every rock on this lofty eminence. The sublime form of the colossal statue of Minerva, the tutelary divinity of Athens, reared its majestic proportions, "towering from the rock of the Acropolis." There were the shrines of all the divinities, the temples of all the gods, the sanctuary of the vengeful furies, and, in full sight, the very gardens where Socrates had poured forth his lessons of wisdom, where Zeno had organized his stern stoical school of philosophy, and where Epicurus had captivated weak humanity with his doctrines of graceful ease or refined sensuality.

Such were the circumstances surrounding the representative of the philosophy and the religion of the Bible. Rising, doubtless, under a full sense of the greatness of his responsibility, Paul uttered that marvelous discourse, in which he exclaims, "O Athenians! I perceive that in all things ye are too superstitious; for as I passed by and beheld your devotions, I found an altar with this inscription, 'To the unknown

God.' Whom, therefore, ye ignorantly worship, Him declare I unto you. God that made the world and all things therein, seeing that He is Lord of heaven and earth, dwelleth not in temples made with hands; neither is worshiped with men's hands, as though He needed any thing: seeing that He giveth to all life, and breath, and all things. Forasmuch, then, as we are the offspring of God, we ought not to think that the Godhead is like unto gold or silver or stone, graven by art and man's device." Your philosophy, O stoics! is false. God's creative energy built this magnificent universe, and God's almighty power guides universal nature. Your divinity, O Epicureans! wrapt in somber abstraction, beholding, from afar, with indifference the affairs of men, is not the divinity of truth; for we also are the offspring of the "unknown God," and in Him we live and move and have our being. Your religion, O priests! is false, and your shrines and splendid temples, and statues of marble and bronze and gold, glittering with precious stones, graven by art and man's device, are but a mockery; for this unknown God, who built the heavens and the earth and who sustaineth all things by the might of His power, dwelleth not in temples made with hands. Turn then, O priests and philosophers! from your idolatry and philosophy, to this unknown God whom ye ignorantly worship; repent, for He hath appointed a day in the which He will judge the world in righteousness.

What response could Pagan philosophy or Pagan idolatry make to this appeal of the Christian hero; and what response can modern philosophy make this day to the same appeal? God has breathed into our nostrils the breath of life, and man has become a living soul. Say what we may, we are the offspring of God, and as His children we are the heirs of immortality; we may defy the Omnipotent and incur His frown, which withers our very being; or we may bring our hearts and souls in unison with God's holiness, and under his beneficent smile be filled with joy and happiness inexpressible and full of glory!

God hath given us the power to scan the universe, to detect its laws, to learn its stupendous organization, to lift the soul of man nearer to

His Divine presence. Where shall the guilty find a refuge? Surely not in the iron—the adamantine laws of physical nature. Suppose, it were possible to endow one of these flying worlds— the earth we inhabit—with a will and a rational soul; and the earth, now an independent, thinking, willing being, should rise in rebellion against the laws of God's control, and refuse longer to obey. The rebellious planet exclaims, Let the sun attract me never so much, I care not for his heat, his light, his life, I refuse to reciprocate the attraction: I have a power of will supreme, my destiny is my own! And thus the fatal decision is made. Slowly the rebel world wheels at each revolution, farther and yet farther from the great center of life and light. In spiral circuit it separates farther and still farther from its wonted path, till finally, cold and darkness and a coming death begin to assert their empire over the misguided world. With a start of horror and a shudder which shakes it to the very center, it now wakes from its dream of independence and exclaims, I will return! I will return! Alas! the return is impossible. The laws of nature are irrevocable. The sun may yet attract with living power the lost wanderer, but the bond is broken, the equilibrium is forever destroyed, and this rebel planet must become a wandering star for which is reserved the blackness of darkness forever!

No, my friends; the analogies of nature, applied to the moral government of God, would crush all hope in the sinful soul. There, for millions of ages, these stern laws have reigned supreme. There is no deviation, no modification, no yielding to the refractory or disobedient. All is harmony, because all is obedience. Close forever, if you will, this strange book claiming to be God's revelation,—blot out forever its lessons of God's creative power, God's superabounding providence, God's fatherhood and loving guardianship to man his erring offspring, and then unseal the leaves of that mighty volume which the finger of God has written in the stars of heaven, and in these flashing letters of living light we read only the dread sentence, "The soul that sinneth it shall surely die!"

www.ingramcontent.com/pod-product-compliance
Lightning Source LLC
Chambersburg PA
CBHW030749230426
43667CB00007B/899